Let There Be Light

A Message
for the Church

Kyle W. Bauer

Copyright © 2019 Kyle W. Bauer

All rights reserved.

Unless otherwise noted, all Scripture quotations are taken from The Holy Bible New King James Version (NKJV), Copyright © 1982 Thomas Nelson, Inc.

ISBN: 978-0-578-20013-2

Dedicated to the Church
who lives by the Light of God's Word

CONTENTS

	Foreword By Jack W. Hayford	1
	Introduction: Awaken to the Light	3
1	A Call to the Light	6
2	Let There Be Light	14
3	Light in the Eyes	23
4	Light in the Heart	40
5	The Armor of Light	46
6	Messengers of Light	54
7	Maintaining the Light	62
8	The Light of Salvation	72
9	Training in the Light	95
10	Meditating in the Light	107
11	The Light and our Worship	139
	About the Author	157

FOREWORD

Among life's greatest joys is the delight of watching your children, and then grandchildren, grow up, marry, and with time, begin their own families. Even more so, is eventually discovering them pursuing the particular pathways that their individual calling and giftings lead them to.

It was deeply heartwarming for me when my grandson Kyle came to me recently and asked me to provide this forward for his book, "Let There Be Light." In response to his request, I joyfully offer the following.

Kyle Bauer, coming from a lineage of fruitful pastors, is a Jesus-following, Bible-centered, Spirit-filled pastor in his own right. Through is careful and meticulous study of the Word of God over many years of training and pastoral ministry, he is truly a worthy candidate for writing a book such as this. This comes as little surprise, seeing as his upbringing was in the climate of a family that honored God and His Word.

It is with great joy, without any reservation, that I recommend this book. You will be enriched and deepened in your understanding of the One who declared Himself to be…The Light of the World.

Dr. Jack W. Hayford, Jr.

Pastor Emeritus,
    The Church On The Way, Van Nuys, CA

Chancellor Emeritus and Founder,
    The King's University, Dallas, TX

INTRODUCTION
AWAKEN TO THE LIGHT

This book was born out of an unexpected experience with an unexpected message in an unexpected place. Some time ago, as I lay my head down on my pillow to sleep, I closed my eyes and was in the place half way between awake and dreaming when, all of a sudden, I heard the voice of the Holy Spirit resounding in my own spirit. Apparently He did not care that I was quite comfortable and nearly lost to sleep. I had not been in prayer nor had been seeking Him. I was simply tired and falling asleep.

He unequivocally said these words:

"My people have My Word, but few of them read it. Tell My people to read their Bibles!"

The time, the place, and the way this message came is in and of itself a metaphor for much of the Church. My dull sleepiness and lack of seeking, and the trumpet-like blast I heard in my spirit are all signs to the Holy Spirit's message to His Church.

When it comes to God's Word and the Church, sadly, many are as drowsy and oblivious spiritually as I was physically. The resounding call is for the Church to awaken to the light of God's Word. In Ephesians 5:14 we are commanded:

"Awake, you who sleep, arise from the dead, and Christ will give you light!"

We are on the verge of the dawning of a New Move of God's grace on the earth. I do not know when or how, but I know it is near. God is calling to His people to awaken from their spiritual slumber, arise from dead works, and be filled with the Light of His uncompromising Word. This is the fundamental preparation for what He desires to unleash on this earth. He needs us to be the Light of the World, and in order to be this, we must be filled with the Light of His Word.

> As God's voice resounded over the dark void,
> So His voice proclaims to His Church today,
>
> "Let There Be Light!"

—Kyle W. Bauer

Let There Be Light

1
A CALL TO THE LIGHT

When I was 20 years old I worked as a facilities maintenance worker at my church. For my first six months on the job I worked the "B shift" from 3:00pm to 11:00pm. The last part of every day was to walk around the property and check every building, turn off every light, and lock every door. Our church facility had a gymnasium and on one particular night I had just turned off all the lights in the gym, but still had to walk the length of the building to leave. There were several tables and chairs set up and the gym was now very dark. I wondered how I was going to negotiate the obstacles in my way without banging my feet or knees on any of them. As I looked around for a moment, I realized the dim, green exit signs threw a faint reflection on the shiny floor, and the shine drew a line straight to me. I knew if I followed line made by the light I would be fine, and if something was in my way I would see its silhouette crossing the light. Following the pathway of light lead me safely through to the other side.

We live in a very dark world filled with all sorts of temptations and evil to trip us up. However, there is great light which will easily dispel any darkness. We are commanded in Ephesians 5:8 to walk as children of the light, and 1 John 1:7 urges us to walk in the light as Jesus is in the light. Yet we cannot walk safely in God's light without stumbling if we do not let it illuminate our path.

God's Word is His light. Psalm 119:105 declares, "Your Word is a lamp unto my feet and a light unto my path." If we will not read it, we are darkening our own steps and jeopardizing our own spiritual safety. Ignoring God's Word is choosing to stumble over every small thing in the way in the darkness, even things that with just a little light could easily be avoided.

God's Word is the beginning of everything: it is light and life. Light and life in God's Word leads us into everything we need. If we will let it shine on us, it will lead us in the "paths of righteousness."

THE GROWING LIGHT

The book of Proverbs is explicit in its call for all people to gain wisdom which comes from the fear of the Lord. In Proverbs, the father—being Solomon, speaks to his "son" and his "child/children." He directly and specifically calls their attention eighteen times in the first eight chapters. Proverbs is a call to us to listen and adhere to the words of our heavenly Father from whom comes all wisdom, knowledge and truth. When such wisdom is obtained, we are told in Proverbs 4:12, "When you walk, you won't be held back; when you run, you won't stumble."

LIFE AT FULL CAPACITY

Walking in the light of our Father's Word will allow us to live life at full throttle and will illuminate our path so we will not be hindered nor stumble in anything. Listen! It is God's good will for us to live our lives at full capacity, fulfilling every dream, running at full speed, and enjoying every minute of it—yet all of this is contingent upon God's Word active, alive, functioning, and guiding every part of our lives.

Proverbs 4:18-19 expounds further on the wisdom and light of God's Word:

> The way of the righteous is like the first gleam of dawn, which shines ever brighter until the full light of day. But the way of the wicked is like total darkness. They have no idea what they are stumbling over.

When we do not walk in the light of God's Word

and wisdom, there is only spiritual darkness and we will stumble over many things in this life. We will stumble over primarily our own ignorance, not to mention satan's tactics designed to cause our downfall. Yet those who walk in the righteousness detailed to us in God's Word, we have more than just a little light, we have light that is continually getting brighter until it shines to its full capacity as the light of the world. The Bible is clear that God's Word active in our lives allows us to run at full speed and shine to our full capacity. It is God's design that the fullness of His Word alive in us brings us into the fullness of His life.

God's Word is the gateway to revival and fullness of life. God's Word shows us how we live. God's Word reveals God's character. God's Word tells us what God requires. God's Word is creative and restorative. God's Word is His Law. God will judge each person according to the standard of His Word. God's Word is spiritual food for us. God's Word is light for our hearts and for the path that lies ahead. We must not allow our feet to stray into the dark, seductive worldviews of the world around us. God is the Creator of life and light. His Word is the path of life and light, and as we walk in this way we will not stumble in darkness. Jesus is calling His Church to come back to the source of light to come back and take His Word seriously and be filled with light.

REVIVAL OF LIGHT[1]

Manasseh was one of the most wicked king to disgrace the kingdom of Judah. He did the most to provoke the Lord to anger than any of the others. He did more evil in God's sight than all the nations whom God destroyed before Israel.[2] He also happened to be the longest reigning king of Judah. His son, Amon, who was equally as wicked, followed him, but his reign was cut short by murder. By the time father and son had died, Judah was on the precipice of God's judgment for their prolonged and profound wickedness. If God judged the previous nations who inhabited the land for their sins, how will He not also judge His own people who had become even more wicked? Israel had sunk into a spiritually dark place.

In the wake of Amon's murder, his eight-year-old son, Josiah, ascended to the throne and unlike his father and grandfather, did what was good and right in God's sight. In the eighteenth year of his reign, he, being only 26 years old, began to repair God's dilapidated and uncared for Temple. It was the beginning of a turn around in the nation. In the midst of the repairs, Hilkiah, the High Priest, found the discarded and forgotten book of the Law which was the original Word God had given to Israel

---

[1] 2 Kings 21-23
[2] 2 Kings 21:9

through Moses. God's Word was read to the king. When Josiah realized what it said and how most of the kings before him had lived, he was terrified recognizing God's coming judgment for Israel's dreadful sins. Josiah grieved for the sins of his people and humbled his heart before God in repentance.

In his zeal for repentance, Josiah immediately undertook a transformation in the land. He cleaned out the Lord's Temple from all idol worship. He violently and passionately eradicated idol worship from the land, purged from Israel all mediums, witches, and sorcerers, restored the Temple, and instituted the observation of the sacred Feasts the Lord had commanded Israel to celebrate. Most of 2 Kings 23 is an account of all Josiah did. The Bible goes on to say, "Now before him there was no king like him, who turned to the Lord with all his heart, with all his soul, and with all his might, according to all the Law of Moses; nor after him did any arise like him."[3] Josiah ushered in one of Israel's greatest revivals—and it was a revival of light.

The impetus for revival, both then and now, is a move of God in great power.

The impetus for God's moving is the repentance from sin.

---

[3] 2 Kings 23:25

The impetus for repentance is genuine grief and anguish over sin.

The impetus for grief over sin is knowledge of what sin is, how it destroys life, and how it breaks God's heart.[4]

The impetus for the knowledge of sin is the light of God's Word.

This is exactly what happened with king Josiah. The light of God's Word showed him good from evil and what God requires of His people, but this revival started with the re-discovery and re-dedication to reading and living God's Word.

God wants to bring revival to every one of our lives and families, and it begins by the re-discovery of the validity, power, and penetrating light of His Word shining into our hearts in such a way that it reveals every corner of darkness and filth to be eradicated. It requires diligence on our part to humble ourselves before the Lord and empty ourselves in utter repentance of anything that is in our lives that is not according to God's Word.

---

[4] See Psalm 51 and how David's heart ached for how he had hurt God and damaged their relationship.

Proverbs 4:20-22
My son, give attention to my words;
Incline your ear to my sayings.
Do not let them depart from your eyes;
Keep them in the midst of your heart;
***For they are life to those who find them,
And health to all their flesh.***

Psalm 119:21, 25
You rebuke the proud—the cursed,
who stray from Your commandments…
My soul clings to the dust;
Revive me according to Your word.

2
LET THERE BE LIGHT

God is Creator, and everything was made by His Word.[5] Word, Spirit, life, and light are all intertwined together at the beginning of creation. The same are also found at the beginning of the New Creation, which John outlines in his Gospel.[6] God is life, His Word brings about creation, and His life is the light of all humanity. Just as God created light in the beginning, He brings light to our darkened lives so that we will shine into the darkness around us as His brand new creations.

His Word gives light and gives life. God's Word and God's Spirit are inextricably linked together. The Hebrew word for "spirit" (ruach) is the same word for "breath" and "wind." Just as our physical words cannot be formed if there is no breath

---

[5] Genesis 1:1-4
[6] John 1:1-5; 20:1

flowing through us, God's Spirit breathes His Word, and His Word brings life and light. There are only two things in the universe that are God-breathed, or created by the breath of God's Spirit[7]: 1) God's Word and 2) human beings. The breath of God in His Word is the very same breath breathed into us.

In fact, John 1 says Jesus was in the beginning with God and is the Word of God. Then the very Word of God became living, human flesh, and this life was the Light of humanity. The Word, Jesus, Life, Light are all one-in-the-same.

> His Word is life to us—it creates.
> His Word is light to us—it defines creation.

LET THERE BE LIGHT[8]
The first four words God speaks in the Bible are, *"Let there be light."*[9] In the utter chaos of the dark and yet-to-be-created world, God calls light into existence as the first order of business. It is interesting that light is introduced before the creation of the planets or stars, implicating that the light God first calls out to is not earthly, physical light. Light is much deeper than what the dictionary

---

[7] 2 Timothy 3:16
[8] Kyle W. Bauer, <u>Watery Grave</u>, copyright 2016, Kyle W. Bauer
[9] Genesis 1:3

says as, "electromagnetic radiation to which the organs of sight react." Light is who God is, and His light is more than something that gives us the ability to see physical objects around us. Light is also spiritual. Everything in the spirit-realm is light. When God calls to the light in Genesis 1:4, He is calling to the spiritual realm. The earth was originally illuminated by His glory, not by the celestial lights.

In those first four loaded words, it is as if God is declaring who He is and what He desires through the creation of light: Let there be the understanding of Me; let there be knowledge; let there be My presence; let there be wisdom; let there be clarity. Such things are the result of spiritual light. The very next verse begins by revealing God's character in this light: the light is good. One cannot create something that is not a part of their being. If the light is good, then the Creator of it is also good.

The very next action God takes is to separate the light from the darkness, (Genesis 1:4). This separation of the two is not merely to give us day and night. In dividing between them, God also gives understanding to whom He is and whom He is not. There is such a thing as light—the good light of the Creator, but there is also such a thing as darkness—and God unequivocally distinguishes between the two. There is good, and there is evil. There is right, and there is wrong. There is illumination, and there is confusion. There is a created order, and there is a perverted order.

In the book of John, the Apostle refers to Jesus as the Word and the Light throughout the Gospel. The two are inseparable, as he writes in John 1:1-5 and 14:

> In the beginning was the Word, and the Word was with God, and the Word was God. He was in the beginning with God. All things were made through Him, and without Him nothing was made that was made. In Him was life, and the life was the light of men. And the light shines in the darkness, and the darkness did not comprehend it…and the Word became flesh and dwelt among us, and we beheld His glory…

Just as God's spoken Word brought the Light into existence in the beginning and brought order to the dark chaos, the opening words to the Gospel of John remind us of the very beginning of creation. In the chaos of a world dark with sin, the same Word and Light became incarnate in Jesus. God's Word and Light, in Jesus Christ, are creating a new beginning for humanity.

It is this same Person who cries out "I am the Light of the world!" (John 8:12). God's Word brings life and light to mankind. In the utter chaos and darkness of a world steeped in sin, God sends the Light of the World, His own Son, Jesus Christ, to help us see life as God intended it to be. The good light of the good Creator illuminates things, not as we wish them to be, but as Creator designed them to be. In the light of Jesus' life, we understand how God designed our lives to function. The theologian C.S. Lewis brilliantly observed, "I believe in Christianity as I believe that the sun has risen: not only because I see it, but because by it I see everything else."

THE DEFINING LIGHT

Nothing in our universe contains any color in and of itself. The color of the shirt you are wearing at this moment is not contained in the essence of the material. If your shirt appears to be blue—it is not actually blue—it is nothing. The science of color tells us that every color of the spectrum is contained in white light. The color that we perceive with our eyes is actually the color in the light spectrum that bounces off an object. Color is light. Hence, where there is no light, all is darkness. If anything had color in and of itself, then darkness would not affect it.

An easy experiment illustrating this fact is to take something green or blue, go into a dark room and shine a red light on it. The object will look black or grayish depending on the hue. Since red light does not have green or blue in its spectrum, no green or blue light is present to bounce off the object.

In a dark world, the Light of Jesus not only shines—*it defines*. In Revelation 19:12, the resurrected Jesus is described with "eyes like flames of fire." Light does not define Jesus, Jesus is the source of the light who gives definition. When we decide to let our world be defined by anything that is not the light of Jesus, we are incapable of seeing any issue as God understands it. Our vision is muddied, unclear, and confused.

As with the experiment with the red light, it is interesting to note how two people can look at the same object, but the light by which the object is illuminated determines their perception of the object. A person who, for instance, looks at the issue of abortion through the light of the world will come to very different conclusions than the person who looks at it through the light of Jesus.

Consider what the prophet Isaiah warns us about devastating consequences walking in a different light, or in the light of our own personal preferences rather than in the clarity God provides:

> Who among you fears the Lord? Who obeys the voice of His Servant? Who walks in darkness and has no light? Let him trust in the

name of the Lord and rely upon his God. Look,
all you who…walk in the light of your
fire…This you shall have from My hand: you
shall lie down in torment. (Isaiah 50:10-11)

Every person has a choice to make: By which light will I choose to walk? There is always another light. There is always a way to try and manipulate the light of God so that one sees what one desires to see. If we do not like all the colors of God's spectrum, we can take the certain colors we like and, like the red light, define everything by it with utter disregard for the ***totality*** of God's revelation. For this reason, there are sectors of the Church that interpret some of God's laws according to current thought when the Bible is clear on the subject. Some desire to twist the light to make it reflect what is most convenient to them.

In the book of Ezekiel, we find one of the most terrifying, non-sugarcoated passages of Scripture regarding the light by which one chooses to walk:

Now some of the elders of Israel came to me
and sat before me. And the word of the Lord
came to me, saying, "Son of man, these men
have set up their idols in their hearts, and put
before them that which causes them to stumble
into iniquity. Should I let Myself be inquired of
at all by them? "Therefore speak to them, and
say to them, 'Thus says the Lord God:

> "Everyone of the house of Israel who sets up his idols in his heart, and puts before him what causes him to stumble into iniquity, and then comes to the prophet, I the Lord will answer him who comes, according to the multitude of his idols…" (Ezekiel 14:1-4)

People set up idols for themselves. They shine the light of their desires, bias, preconceived ideas, and selfish ambitions upon everything they do. People do this so well that they will actually persuade themselves that the light of their own will is indeed the light of God's will. Where there is stubbornness, lack of repentance, and self-will, God will allow a person to continue in their darkness while they continue believing they walk in God's light.

A prime example of choosing to walk in one's own light comes from the much-venerated father of psychiatry, Sigmund Freud, who understood well the problem of human depression, yet whose ultimate solution turned out to be a different kind of light. Freud writes that one of the sources of human depression is that humanity is incapable of attaining the moral standards set for us. This produces a feeling of inadequacy, guilt, shame, and thus, depression. It is worth noting that the moral standards at the time of Freud's writing were quite different than they are today. Part of this decline of standards has to do with Freud's next proposition.

Sadly, Freud was on the cusp of stumbling onto the brilliant solution God had given humanity when he went the opposite way. Freud was right in his analysis that humanity cannot attain God's righteous, moral standards. This is why God sent Jesus Christ to fulfill them and die for our sins so that in Him we can live as God wants. That is the message of the Gospel! God has done for us what none of us could do on our own.

Freud's solution was not in Christ, but rather to change the standards! In other words, if we cannot live up to the standard, then let us redefine the standard to our liking. Who defines the standards, anyway? When I get to define the standards—then I can never be wrong! Problem solved. Actually, there is a much greater problem created—it is a redefinition of the light. God is the ultimate standard—He is the definition of the light by which we live.

3
LIGHT IN THE EYES

Have you ever seen a person with eyes that are alive? A pregnant woman who is glowing with the anticipation of new life; a new bride; a happy, confident person? What about someone who has "dead eyes"? Maybe a severely depressed person or a mug shot of an unrepentant criminal. There is something is very telling in the eyes. The Bible describes them as "the lamp of the body."[10] Whatever is in us fills us with either light or darkness and it is perceptible to people. The light with which we fill ourselves and by which we walk shows through the eyes; the windows of the soul.

The life, wisdom, presence, glory, holiness, purity, Word and person of God is represented in light, after all, He is "the Father of lights, with whom

---

[10] Matthew 6:22

there is no variation or shadow of turning." He is also the God "who dwells in unapproachable light."[11] The light of God Himself fills us and refracts out of us—as He is, so we too are to be: the light of the world! This light is God's Word. As Ephesians 1:17-18a tells us, "that the God of our Lord Jesus Christ, the Father of glory, may give to you the spirit of wisdom and revelation in the knowledge of Him, the *eyes* of your understanding being *enlightened*..." As we move through this book together studying the light of God's Word, allow the Holy Spirit to fill your heart, eyes, and mind with the power of the Word of God.

THE WORD OF GOD IS PURITY
"The words of the Lord are pure words, like silver tried in a furnace of earth, purified seven times."[12] Purity also defines the Word of God. The comparison of God's Word being purified seven times in a crucible means that there is no imperfection in it whatsoever.

God's Word is far deeper and more mysterious than we know. There are secrets and hidden treasures in the Bible that God is willing to reveal to those who fear Him.[13] "Purified seven times" also indicates the different layers of understanding within God's

---

[11] James 1:17; 1 Timothy 6:16
[12] Psalm 12:6
[13] Psalm 25:14 (NKJV)

Word which He makes known to us the more we develop an intimate friendship with Him. I once heard a preacher challenge his listeners to take time with God's Word and ask the Holy Spirit to give us seven different revelations on each and every verse. Have you ever read a passage of Scripture many times, and still had new insight into it? Have you ever heard a preacher speak on a familiar verse and still bring out of it something totally new? Even Jesus said studying God's Word is like discovering treasures both old and new![14] Just imagine how purified our lives would be if we filled ourselves up with something as clean as God's Word!

The blood of Jesus forgives us, but it is the Word of God that examines us, decontaminates us, and teaches us how to live in the way that pleases God. If we will live by His Word and be purified by it, there will be less and less contaminants in our lives that hinder us drawing closer to God's presence. His Word points out areas of sin in our lives with the purpose of forming us presentable to God and making us into a place God wants to live. Jesus furthered this concept of closeness with God by saying when we obey His Word, He will make His home in us and will manifest Himself to us.[15] As we consume His Word, it begins to work its own purity

---

[14] Matthew 13:52
[15] John 14:21

inside of us and we become people of holiness, righteousness, and justice and a purified temple where He wants to take up residence.

In this same vein, Jesus affirmed His disciples in John 15:3, "You are already clean because of the word which I have spoken to you." It is by Jesus' words He purifies His people. Before His incarnation, Jesus was known as the "Word of God."[16] Jesus is the Word of God made flesh and His words are those of the light and purity of God Himself. His life "was the light of man."

Ephesians 5:25-27 furthers this concept of God's pure Word:

> Husbands, love your wives, just as Christ also loved the church and gave Himself for her, that He might sanctify and cleanse her ***with the washing of water by the word***, that He might present her to Himself a glorious church, not having spot or wrinkle or any such thing, but that she should be holy and without blemish.

The context of these verses is that of the Apostle Paul talking not as much about marriage as he is of the great mystery of the Church as the Bride of Christ. The earthly image of marriage is only a

---

[16] John 1:1

shadow of what God desires with His people. Just as brides wear white as a symbol of purity, so Jesus will receive to Himself a bride—a Church—without any filth. Sooner or later we will see Jesus face-to-face. Either He will come back for us or we will die and step into His presence. Either way, He wants us to be pure, clean, holy, and ready. The way He prepares His Church to be the pure, covenant partner He requires is to wash her with the purity of His Word. As we intake His Word, we become pure as He is pure.

THE WORD OF GOD IS LIGHT

As we spoke about last chapter, God created the natural light by which we live from His spoken Word. The light was good and pure as surely as its Maker is good and pure.

1 John 1:5,
> This is the message which we have heard from Him and declare to you, that ***God is light*** and in Him is no darkness at all.

2 Corinthians 4:4, 6,
> ...whose minds the god of this age has blinded, who do not believe, lest the light of the gospel of the glory of Christ, who is the image of God, should ***shine*** on them...For it is the God who commanded light to shine out of darkness, who has shone in our hearts to give ***the light of the***

knowledge of the glory of God in the face of Jesus Christ.

The Gospel of Jesus Christ is light! The same God who spoke, "Let there be light" into the darkness is the God who speaks His Word into the darkness of our lives and, by His Word, cries, "Let there be light!" As His light shines upon our hearts, we begin to live by the light of the Gospel He gives. The light of the Gospel of Jesus illuminates the deficiencies of our lives so that we can be cleaned, purified, and acceptable people among whom to dwell.

THE WORD OF LIGHT AND PURITY

The Bible brings even more depth and clarity to these truths. The purity and light of God's Word are not separate concepts, they are deeply intertwined as we see in Psalm 19:8 and Malachi 3:2:

> The statutes of the Lord are right, rejoicing the heart; the commandment of the Lord is ***pure, enlightening*** the eyes...

> But who can endure the day of His coming? And who can stand when He appears? For He is like a ***refiner's fire and like launderers' soap***.

Psalm 19:8 speaks of God's Word as both purity

and giving light to the person in such a way that even their eyes reflect the transformation God's Word brings them. I am sure you have known people (and perhaps you are this person!) of whom others say, "there is something different about you!" That is the light in the eyes! When God's Word comes into a person with purity and the freedom only His truth can bring about in our lives, there is a blessed, happy heart, and the light of God's presence, wisdom, love, and purity in the eyes!

The verse in Malachi was written roughly 400 years before the coming of Jesus, and this prophecy speaks directly to the day of Jesus' ministry. Just as John the Baptist said that Jesus would "baptize…with fire," so Malachi prophecies the same process and baptism of holiness and refinement. It is the fire that refines and the soap that purifies.

Yet where there is fire there is also light, and for soap to have its full effect, there must be water. Malachi is saying that when the Messiah comes, there will be fire and soap; light and water—and BOTH indicate the process of purification—this is the job of God's Word. We must read it!

In Psalm chapter 1 we see clearly how meditating on God's Word brings God's presence and light to the eyes.

This first Psalm is the great set up for the entire book of Psalms. The Holy Spirit, who composed the Bible over a period of 1,500 years, did not just happen throw this book carelessly together. As with everything God does, Psalm 1 is intentionally written and placed. In biblical interpretation, we have to pay attention to certain things like the "firsts." The way something is first set up, or the way a concept or a word is first used is an indication of the importance of it for the rest of the book or the spiritual concept developed throughout the Bible.

The Psalms is a book of prophecy, intimacy with God, worship, praise, prayer and the pouring out one's heart before God. God designed the entire book of Psalms to bring us the blessing of His presence. The premise on which the Psalms begin is to love and meditate on God's Word. Most everything in the Psalms has to do with the Word of God, loving it, trusting it, and living it.

PSALM 1: GOD'S WORD IN DAILY LIFE

With the understanding of God's Word as light and purity, we now come to Psalm 1:1-2. Read it aloud:

> Blessed is the man who walks not in the counsel of the ungodly, nor stands in the path of sinners, nor sits in the seat of the scornful;

but his delight is in the law of the Lord, and in His law he meditates day and night.

The entire book of Psalms begins by telling us how we can live a live blessed by God. Who doesn't want that?! The blessed and happy person is one who does not:

Walk in the counsel of the wicked,
Stand in the way of sinners,
Sit in the seat of mockers.

The words ***walk, stand, and sit*** in the Hebrew, as well as in English, are very common words. In fact, two of these words are used more than 500 times in the Old Testament and one word used more than 1,000 times. There is nothing overly noteworthy about these words. As I studied these words, I remembered that it has been well over a decade since I took Hebrew class, and these words are so common that I still remembered them with little difficulty from my seminary days. The mundane commonality of these words speaks to our daily lives. We find strength in God, purity, holiness, and light, in moments of worshipful ecstasy, however it is in ordinary, everyday moments where we learn to live out the reality of God's Word.

The way we are walking, standing, and sitting is found in the hundreds of daily, common decisions we make. The way we choose to respond in a tough situation, the we speak to co-workers, what we choose to entertain ourselves with. Our everyday ways of living and thinking, the people we choose to associate with and have speak into our lives can either contaminate or purify us depending on whether we walk in the counsel of God's Word or the counsel of the wicked. The Psalm is clear: joy and happiness come from a life of righteousness as God defines it, not as we would design it.

Along with these three verbs, there are three corresponding nouns: ***wicked***, ***sinners***, and ***mockers***. When we look a little deeper into the meaning of each of these three descriptions, they have to do with people who laugh at holy things, who are morally impure, and who are wrongdoers and guilty of sin. This definition stands for people of this kind whether they realize it or not. These three words are also of very common usage. Just as walk, stand, and sit have to do with daily life and habits, so do wicked, sinners, and mockers deal with daily attitudes, words, habits, or decisions we make of whether or not we will decide to live in what is good, right, and just, or wicked, sinful, and mocking.

Where do we walk, stand, and sit? What and where do we find ourselves doing, thinking, watching, and saying during the day. How many times do we sit in front of YouTube for hours and watching "mockers" and "sinners" while we laugh with them? How many times do we stand around and gather the latest gossip? We have all been guilty of this.

What was the last website you visited? What did you look at? Was it morally pure according to God's standards or was is questionable? How many times have we looked at unworthy things and in so doing have participated with them? What do we read? What do we laugh at? What do we move and dance to? What exclamatory expressions most naturally come out of our mouths in a moment of surprise, frustration, or anger? Are they curse words? Are they blasphemous words against God? All of these are daily decisions that determine if we walk, stand, or sit in sin. This does not necessarily mean that the person who walks, stands, or sits with such sinners is the origin of the sin, but walking, standing, and sitting with them does implicate us in the sin. Those who participate, even by watching or listening, are equally as guilty. Even just watching or saying nothing when ugly, unworthy things are being talked about is giving approval.

However, the closer we walk with the Holy Spirit, the unworthy things of this world have less and less hold on us. Knowing God's Word and having constant and growing friendship with the Holy

Spirit makes it so much easier to resist temptation and to identify those things which have no spiritual or eternal value. Such things no longer interest us the same way they used to, in fact, they begin to even disgust us. Now God's purity is living in us through the instruction of His Word and we have found our "delight in the law of the Lord." Happy is such a person!

Psalm 1 continues to instruct us on what makes for a happy and blessed person. Such people:

Delight in the law of the Lord.
Meditate on God's Word day and night.

The blessed person avoids sin and sinful people and finds sustenance, instruction, delight, and joy in consuming God's Word. I love that the entire book of Psalms begins with the word "blessed." This is the message of the Psalms. Blessing comes through trust in God and adherence to His Word, while rejection of God's Word leads to a life far from His eternal blessings and joy.

The New Living Translation begins this same Psalm by saying, "Happy is the person…" I love that! The Word of God not only refines and purifies—it also gives joy, happiness and blessing! Remember Psalm 19:8, "The statutes of the Lord are right, ***rejoicing the heart***…!" This kind of happiness and joy are available only to those who live in the blessings that God's Word provides. That is not to say that someone who has never read the Bible cannot experience happiness, but there is a level of pure joy and blessedness that comes from the throne of God that those living outside of God cannot experience—it is a supernatural joy.

The next words of this Psalm instruct us on how to obtain and live in this supernatural joy that only comes from God. The word "delight" in the Hebrew is equally as common as the other words we have already looked at. Once again, this speaks to the daily delight found in relationship with God and meditation on His Word which gives us purity and light. Those that meditate on God's Word day and night and refuse to participate in the ways of life and belief systems and entertainment of sin, are those who will receive God's blessing on their lives. Living in God's Word, presence, and joy is like exercise and training. It is difficult to begin because we have trained ourselves to "delight" in lesser things. But the closer we get to God, the more the desire and joy grows. Joy grows because we were made for relationship with God. I reiterate, ***the person who does not meditate on God's Word cannot enter into God's fullest blessings nor can they know God's fullest joy.***

PEOPLE OF SUBSTANCE

For those who avoid sin and allow God's Word to purify and enlighten them, God gives deeper promises than only those of happiness and blessing. God promises to make us into weighty, authoritative, valuable, and fruitful people of enduring substance in all we do. We stand to inherit all of the eternal glory and rulership of Heaven. Psalm 1:3-6 continues:

> He shall be like a tree planted by the rivers of water, that brings forth its fruit in its season, whose leaf also shall not wither; and whatever he does shall prosper. The ungodly are not so, but are like the chaff which the wind drives away. Therefore the ungodly shall not stand in the judgment, nor sinners in the congregation of the righteous. For the Lord knows the way of the righteous, but the way of the ungodly shall perish.

Delighting in and meditating on God's Word—the Word that gives light and purifies—comes with the promise of stability, strength, and fruitfulness. A tree's deep roots give it stability and strength in the fiercest of storms, and the healthy tree is fruitful in every season. Likewise, we are to be rooted and grounded in God's Word which will fill us with God's fruitful blessings and glory. The Hebrew word "glory" (chabod) carries the idea of the "weight" wealth, honor, authority, and position. In the same way, a life filled with God's Word is that which has spiritual "weight" like a tree weighed down with fruit.

The idea of stability, strength, and fruitfulness is one of God's great blessings to those who will adhere to His Word. As we grow in our faith (and faith comes by hearing, and hearing *by the Word of God*[17]), our lives will be transformed to be aligned with God's qualities and in step with His character. Such transformative qualities promise that we "will neither be barren nor unfruitful"[18] in our lives. These are the same people the book of Revelation calls "overcomers." We carry the promise of becoming what Jesus will make us. Psalm 1 says we will be as healthy, strong, substantive trees, and Revelation 3:12 says, "***I will make [you] a pillar in the temple of my God.***" Both trees and pillars are large, strong, and stable. Trees grow and pillars are formed—in other words, ***both have a process of becoming.***

We who will delight in God's Word and allow its light to purify us, God is making, forming, and transforming us into what He designed us to be, and His design for us in *limitless*. We must not rob ourselves of the wonders and mysteries of God's

---

[17] Romans 10:17
[18] 2 Peter 1:8

glory, destiny, delights, and eternity for us by ignoring His Word. His Word contains everything we need to grow to become people of limitless joy, power, understanding, relationship, love, goodness, and worth. It is all ours if we will live by His Word.

But not the sinners, wicked, and mockers. They are the opposite. They are like thin chaff the wind blows away. Chaff is the papery substance that envelops grain. To separate the grain from the chaff, the winnowers toss the grain up in the air and let the breeze carry away the inedible chaff. Such is the description of those who will not live by God's Word. Their lives are empty and fruitless according to Heaven's standards. Just as the chaff is inedible, there is nothing of spiritual substance or eternal value to the lives they have created with their own wisdom and cunning. They have no weight, no heavenly glory or honor to them, and as such, when they stand before God, they will have nothing to offer Him. Unlike the weight of fruit, with a simple breath of God at His judgment, their nothingness and the lack of weighty value, their lives are puffed away. Take note of what 1 Corinthians 3:12-15 says regarding this very concept:

> Now if anyone builds on this foundation with gold, silver, precious stones, wood, hay, straw, each one's work will become clear; for the Day *[of judgment]* will declare it,

because it will be revealed by fire; and the fire will test each one's work, of what sort it is. If anyone's work which he has built on it endures, he will receive a reward. If anyone's work is burned, he will suffer loss; but he himself will be saved, yet so as through fire.

With what are you building your life? Are you building for the temporal or the eternal? Are you storing up treasure in heaven, or is your treasure only here on earth?[19] God is looking for only those whose lives produce eternal results, and that is a life which is built by God's Word. Building for eternity is living by God's Word which purifies us from the things of this world and gives us the light of His wisdom and presence so that we know how to build a life that pleases Him.

> Unless the LORD builds the house,
> They labor in vain who build it.
> Psalm 127:1

---

[19] Matthew 6:20; 19:21

4
LIGHT IN THE HEART

I have had the privilege of pastoring people for going on two decades. Pastoring is both wonderfully fulfilling and strangely perplexing at the same time. People have surprised me many times filling me with both amazing joy and deep pain; admiration and bewilderment. There is a saying in Spanish I have come to appreciate as both insightful, cautionary, and instructional to those who are perceptive and honest with themselves: "Faces we see, hearts we do not."

Too many times have I been taken in by the outward appearance of piety, faith, religion, and goodness. People look upon the outward appearance, and all too often judge by the same, but the Lord looks at the heart.[20] God's light penetrates to the heart and reveals its actual state. The heart is where our true beliefs, intents, motives, treasures,

---

[20] 1 Samuel 16:7

and worldviews dwell.

A look on the face can hide the motive of the heart, but, in time, it is through our actions where the true essence of our worldview leaks out. This is what is most perplexing as a pastor. Many people do and say the right things, but the actions of their lives give away the true intent of the heart. They desire right living, but so many times they go on making the opposite decisions out of desperation or fear. As my father once told me, "When you make a decision in fear, it is *always* the wrong decision."

Jesus felt this same bewilderment with the religious community of Israel in His day when He declared to them, "This people honors me with their lips, but their heart is far from me."[21] The wonderful thing about the light of God's Word is it does not merely shine on the surface—it penetrates to the heart. The light of the sun shows on the face of a person, but the heart remains hidden. The light of God's Word shines into the darkness of the human soul, and nothing is hidden. His light separates good and evil, and divides between soul and spirit, joints and marrow, and it discerns the thoughts and intents of the heart.[22]

I have dealt with many people, who, having served

---

[21] Matthew 15:8
[22] Hebrews 4:12

the Lord for many years, been faithful at church, made great shows of piety and religiosity, in a moment of desperation or pure fleshliness, make horrible life decisions that end up having dramatic effects on their lives, faith, and even their own ability to live in honesty, integrity, truth, and victory as followers of Jesus Christ: The Christian man who sleeps with and tries to marry a woman, who turned out to be a witch, because she was a pretty face and he really wanted to be married; the girl who is waiting patiently and faithfully for God to bring her a husband and ends up sleeping with another "Christian" man from church; the church woman who turns to a warlock to curse her husband after finding out that he was unfaithful to her; people who allow their children to act out as the opposite gender; men, who after coming to church, beat their wives; those who defy their pastor and talk bad about him after a loving confrontation; countless Christian parents who allow their children to be instructed in the arts of witchcraft at an introductory level by Harry Potter; the eagerness with which many Christians around the world adapt to the changing cultural climate regarding homosexuality and other cultural fads of destruction. These are only a few examples of countless other stories—all of them true—and all of them done by people in the Church.

How can there be such spiritual dullness and

darkness among those who supposedly live in God's light? Why do so many in the Church, purported servants of Christ, the very same who love declaring that they are "more than conquerors" in Jesus Christ, live this way? It is at best ignorance, and at worst brazen defiance of God. But the fact remains that God's Word is not being allowed to shine deep into the soul. Darkness muddies thoughts, obscures spiritual realities, and blinds us to the right ways of living that God requires, whereas God's light would reveal and change ouractions.

Israel, God's chosen people, constantly exchanged their relationship with God for idols. They rejected the light of God's purity and righteousness (literally, the "rightness" of living) for the dark filthiness of sin. God brings this charge against His own people through the prophet Hosea saying:

> "There is no faithfulness, no kindness,
>   no knowledge of God in your land.
> You make vows and break them;
>   you kill and steal and commit adultery.
> There is violence everywhere—
>   one murder after another…[23]

Hosea points out that very reason such sin persisted among God's people was because there was no

---

[23] Hosea 4:1-2 (NLT)

understanding or knowledge of God. Jesus Himself, in reference to those who continue to follow God throughout the ages, said that in the End Times, because lawlessness abounds, the love of many will grow cold.[24]

Lawlessness is not another word for anarchy. What Jesus is saying is that where there is either disdain for or ignorance of God's laws, even those who loved the Lord can fall away. The prophet Hosea continues saying, "My people are destroyed for lack of knowledge."[25] The lawlessness and lack of knowledge of God disallow the heart to be transformed into one that pleases God.

Without such light shining in our hearts, we cannot be changed. The Bible is what ***shows us*** the way to be saved from sin and ***keeps us*** in the way of salvation so we do not return to the way of sin. Where there is a lack of knowledge, the people will perish in their sin—even those who claim belief in Jesus. It is no longer acceptable for the people of God to put on a godly face that is inconsistent with a non-transformed heart. "Faces we see, hearts we do not," but God will judge even our secret life.[26] God's Word will transform us to be people whose faces and actions are consistent with the

---

[24] Matthew 24:12
[25] Hosea 4:6
[26] Romans 2:16 (NLT)

genuineness of the new heart His is creating in us and this is predicated on the light of His Word shining in us.

> Joyful are people of integrity,
> who follow the instructions of the Lord.
> Joyful are those who obey his laws
> and search for him with all their hearts.
> They do not compromise with evil,
> and they walk only in his paths.
> You have charged us
> to keep your commandments carefully.
> ***Oh, that my actions would consistently***
> ***reflect your decrees!***
> ***Then I will not be ashamed***
> ***when I compare my life with your commands.***
> As I learn your righteous regulations,
> I will thank you by living as I should![27]

---

[27] Psalm 119:1-7 (NLT)

5
THE ARMOR OF LIGHT

Some time ago I preached a long series of messages about the Armor of God and came to a wonderful conclusion about the connection between the Armor and the power of the Word of God. There is an amazing connection between God's Word, light, goodness, and His divine purposes on the earth and the pieces of the Armor of God.

The most famous passage of the Armor of God is found in Ephesians 6:10-17. This passage speaks of each piece of armor as salvation, faith, righteousness, truth, peace, and the Word of God as protection for us against the works of the devil. Yet this is not the only place the concept of God's Armor is found. Romans 13:12 also says, "The night is far spent, the day is at hand. Therefore let us cast off the works of darkness, and let us put on the _armor of light_."

It is instructive for us to see the Armor of God as also the Armor of Light. Both types of armor are protection against the evil that would destroy us, and raiment of light that shines in the darkness of our hearts to produce God's goodness and whose luster pushes back the shadows of the devil's kingdom in our world. The Bible continues to develop the properties of this armor of light: "For this light within you produces only what is good and right and true,"[28] and "The light shines in the darkness, and the darkness has not overcome it."[29]

The Armor of Light is to destroy the darkness and allow the fullness of God's Word to bring understanding where there is none. It illuminates our own hearts in order to expose all that which is contrary to His way of being and living. The Armor of God both protects us from evil and exposes evil residing in us. His Armor is His Word.

Isaiah 59 gives us a window into Israel's story of failure and redemption in conjunction with the working of God's armor. God rescued Israel so they would be His people and reflect Him to the world. But God gives a scathing rebuke to Israel for living contrary to His Word, indeed contrary to the very reason for which He brought them into existence.

---

[28] Ephesians 5:9 (NLT)
[29] John 1:5 (NIV)

God indicts his people throughout this chapter because there is no justice, no *righteousness*, no *truth*, no *peace*, no *faith*, God's *Word* is not being followed, nor is God's *salvation* being lived out.[30] In fact, the opening verses declare that God's arm is not short so that it cannot save,[31] yet God's people did not live in His salvation because of their great sins. In other words, they chose to walk in the exact opposite way God showed them.

It is interesting to note that the very things God describes as missing among His people in Isaiah 59, are the very pieces of armor detailed for us in Ephesians 6: The helmet of *salvation*, the breastplate of *righteousness*, the belt of *truth*, the shoes of *peace*, the shield of *faith,* and the sword of the *word* of God. The virtues God expected of Israel are the very same pieces of Armor He gives us to spiritually protect ourselves. This point cannot be overstated! When we walk according to God's Word, there is protection for our lives and souls.

The Armor of God is the very character of God, and God's character is exemplified in His Word. Interestingly, we see both the character of the Armor of God and the Armor of Light missing in Israel as the prophet bemoans in this same passage,

---

[30] Isaiah 59:2-15
[31] Isaiah 59:1

"We look for light, but all is darkness; for brightness, but we walk in deep shadows."[32]

Instead of adhering to God's Word, in which is found His goodness, holiness, and light—really His very character—the people had become spiritually dull and dark being given to violence, perversion, murder, injustice, and lies all the while claiming exceptional status as God's holy, chosen people. Because Israel would not dress themselves with God's character nor walk in His light, they became exposed to God's vengeance and punishment instead of living God's good plan for them, which was for them to know His peace, provision, light, and salvation.

There are consequences for sin; the price of sin is always death. In other words, the lack of the knowledge of the Word of God produced a life of sin which precluded them from the life, salvation, and protection of God. In their love for sin, the people God had chosen, chose to make themselves His enemies.

The darkness of sin has nothing to do with goodness and holiness—they are exact opposites. Nevertheless, God's salvation, righteousness, peace, and truth, _will go forth_, and they _will be_

---

[32] Isaiah 59:9

implemented on the earth.

If God's people will not dress themselves with the Armor of His salvation, righteousness, peace, and truth, in order to make them known on earth, then God will apply them against His own people. Ironically, the virtues that were to be their protection became their undoing. Isaiah 59:15-18 says:

> Then the Lord saw it, and it displeased Him that there was no justice. He saw that there was no man, and wondered that there was no intercessor; therefore His own arm brought salvation for Him; and His own righteousness, it sustained Him. For He put on righteousness as a breastplate, and a helmet of salvation on His head; He put on the garments of vengeance for clothing, and was clad with zeal as a cloak. According to their deeds, accordingly He will repay, fury to His adversaries, recompense to His enemies…

The imagery is unequivocal—God desired His people to live in such a way to give them victory, but their sin made them God's enemies and put them in a precarious position to receive God's judgment. God dressed Himself as a warrior and donned the Armor of His own virtue. He Himself will bring about the destruction of sin and His goodness will prevail whereas He had intended to do so alongside His people who were to have been clothed with the same virtue. By punishing the enemies of His goodness, He will produce a people who live by His Word and who will actively produce faith, righteousness, peace, truth, and salvation on earth. Israel refused to walk by His Word, but eradication of evil is what God has already determined will happen. His Armor is for our protection, but if any of His people refuse it, they will be turned against them in judgment.

Every believer beware, God's standards apply across the board to believers and unbelievers alike, and judgment begins in His own house.[33] We are to examine ourselves constantly to be sure we remain in the faith and completely faithful to God in all things,[34] and walking in His full protection and light.

The Armor of God is the representation of God's good character—the very same character we see in the light of His good creation, and the very same we are to imitate and live out as His people. One way or another God will cause His purposes and goodness to be known on the earth, but He is restoring to us "the image of His Son,"[35] and has

---

[33] 1 Peter 4:17
[34] 2 Corinthians 13:5
[35] Romans 8:29

equipped us with the Armor of His salvation, righteousness, truth, peace, faith and Spirit in order to carry out His purposes on the earth. Creation itself groans and cries out waiting for the revealing of the children of God.[36] All things will begin to come back into order as God's people walk in His light and His character as His mature, obedient people.

As one studies the Armor of Light, it becomes evident that the essential component of each of the pieces of Armor is the light of God's Word:

- How do we come to know about _salvation_ in Jesus Christ? The Word of God.[37]
- How do we know what _righteousness_ is and how to live in it? The Word of God.[38]
- How do we know spiritual _truth_? The Word of God.[39]
- How do we come to _faith_? The Word of God.[40]
- How do we have _peace_? The Word of God.[41]
- What is the spiritual _sword_ with which we lay waste the enemy? The Word of God.[42]

---

[36] Romans 8:19
[37] Ephesians 2:8-9
[38] Psalm 119:1-8
[39] Psalm 119:105
[40] Romans 10:17
[41] Philippians 4:7
[42] Ephesians 6:17

The Word of God protects us from every evil scheme of the devil, keeps us from living in the flesh and living in the light, and teaches us to live victoriously in Jesus Christ. There is no substitute for the Word of God being constantly inputted into our lives. There is no substitute for personal, daily reading the Bible: it both ***shows us*** and ***keeps us*** on the road to salvation.

6
MESSENGERS OF LIGHT

The first chapter of the book of James holds some marvelous truths about the power of the light of God's Word. He gives us a furthered understanding and appreciation for its work in our hearts, which will keep us from everything that will destroy our lives.

> God blesses those who patiently endure testing and temptation. Afterward they will receive the crown of life that God has promised to those who love him. And remember, when you are being tempted, do not say, "God is tempting me." God is never tempted to do wrong, and he never tempts anyone else. Temptation comes from our own desires, which entice us and drag us away. These desires give birth to sinful

actions. And when sin is allowed to grow, it gives birth to death. So don't be misled, my dear brothers and sisters. Whatever is good and perfect is a gift coming down to us from God our Father, who created all the lights in the heavens. He never changes or casts a shifting shadow. Of His own will He brought us forth by the word of truth, that we might be a kind of firstfruits of His creatures.[43]

It is immensely interesting that in his discourse on not being lead into sin, James refers to God as the creator of all lights and He never changes nor casts a shadow. God is the Creator of light and no sin is in Him. His light is good and can be trusted to lead us into the right ways of living.

Though this passage ends by telling us we were begotten by the truth of His Word, in reality, the Word of God has everything to do with this entire passage of Scripture, not just the ending.

Earlier in this same chapter,[44] James tells us the testing of our faith, through many different tribulations, perfects us as believers. In spite of the fact James uses the same Greek word for temptations as he does for trials, it is clear that *trials*

---

[43] James 1:12-18
[44] James 1:2-4

in this life test the genuineness of our faith, but devilish *temptations* are designed to derail genuine faith. Difficult times that *refine* a person are vastly different from the outright demonic or fleshly seduction to sin which will *destroy* a person. Either way, trial or temptation, these are proving grounds to see the strength or weakness of our faith.

The very first temptation happened when satan seduced the woman to eat of the fruit God forbade her and her husband to eat.[45] James is clear that sin and temptation come from our own desires. Satan does indeed tempt—he did so with Jesus—yet satan cannot obligate us to do anything we do not wish to do. The old adage "the devil made me do it" is simply not true. Nor does the excuse of, "Well, I am just a person with needs. How am I supposed to resist? I am only human!" hold any water. We have been crucified with Christ and Christ lives in us[46] and He who lives in us in greater than the one who lives in the world![47] Temptation is not sin, but giving in to temptation is sin. Since no one can make us sin by giving in to temptation, then whose fault is it when we participate? None but our own. Ultimately the woman wanted the fruit for herself. Her fleshly desires won the day. She could have simply walked away or rebuked the serpent since

---

[45] Genesis 3:1-6
[46] Galatians 2:20
[47] 1 John 4:4

she and her husband had dominion over "every creeping thing that creeps on the earth."[48] But instead of walking in her God-given authority, she gave it away when she sinned.

MESSENGERS OF LIGHT
In the midst of the temptation, the Bible says a rather revealing thing about what causes people to fall into sin. *"...the woman saw that the tree was **good** for food, that it was **pleasant** to the eyes, and a tree **desirable** to make one wise..."[49]* Most of the time sin does not show itself to us as blatantly evil rather it shows up with an aspect of goodness and desirability. If satan showed up on your doorstep looking like evil incarnate, there is little chance you would go with him to commit evil. But evil wraps itself as something good, pleasant, and desirable. Too many people are taken in by the surface-level innocence of someone or something—if it looks and feels good, then it must be good. But not all that glitters is gold. Many things that have the appearance of good actually hide a demonic nature. The woman saw that the fruit was good and she took it, but at its core was a satanic lie that caused her and her husband to lose everything.

Who doesn't want love? Of course we all do. As a matter of fact, God is love. So love, in all its forms

---
[48] Genesis 1:26
[49] Genesis 3:6

must win. Isn't that the mantra of today's culture? It sounds good. It sounds right. Therefore, if you don't want certain aspects of "love" to win, then you must be a person of hate. This is nothing more than a lie wrapped with an aspect of goodness, and millions of people, including many followers of Christ, have fallen for it. The wrapping paper of goodness, sensitivity, and "love" cover the demonic lie of homosexuality and mistaken sexual identity, yet many people have not the spiritual adeptness to see it for what it is.

I have recently been astounded at how many Christian families, with both parents and kids alike, having such an affinity for Harry Potter. "It is only fiction and fantasy, and a good story," they say. Yet their spiritual dullness disallows them to see beneath the surface for what it is: An introduction to witchcraft. Isn't the story about a boy who goes to a school for wizardry and witchcraft? Since when is this acceptable for a follower of Christ? Is it possible something as such a "good and pleasant" story could be a demonic ploy that takes the edge off our spiritual senses and even arouse a curiosity in our children for spiritual things of a dark nature? The Harry Potter franchise further sell a cast-a-spell workbook for children in which they can advance into witchcraft. Don't try to explain this away as a fantasy story. It has demonic deception and traps behind it trying to seduce and warp an entire generation.

God's Word is a lamp to our feet and a light unto our path.[50] It shows us the way of salvation, and keeps us firmly on the path. But 2 Corinthians 11:14 tells us that the devil masquerades himself as an angel of light, and in the aspect of goodness, many people are led astray. The Greek word *angelos* is not defined as simply an angelic spirit, it is defined as a "messenger." In other words, satan comes as a messenger bearing light, albeit a different light; a light that does not burn out the darkness, but distracts from the darkness behind it, or a light which disallows one to see the true, full color realities of what they are looking at. Not every word is to be trusted. We are to distinguish everything around us by the light that God's Word gives, not by any other light, even if it be a "angel of light."

There are many who come with deceiving miracles. Yes, we are talking about real, supernatural miracles which will deceive many people. The devil has spiritual power, but God's power is far greater. The devil's power is a falsification of the real deal. Our church functions in the supernatural and the power gifts of the Holy Spirit, but one must judge what is going on behind whatever works are happening by the light of God's Word. Are people being saved and loving Jesus more? Then the works

---

[50] Psalm 119:105

are from the Lord.

Remember in the courts of Pharaoh, Jannes and Jambres used demonic powers to duplicate some of the miracles Moses performed by the power of God.[51] There are miracles that look good, but beneath the surface have a deceptive and demonic nature. Paul tells the Galatians that even if an angel was to pronounce to them a different gospel, they were to not believe it![52] Jesus Himself told us that many false prophets will come to deceive many[53] —this includes the deception of many Christians.

In this same passage James goes on to tell us not to be deceived. Deceived by what? We can be easily deceived by our own personal interpretation of what is good when we try and find it outside of God. "Every *good gift*…is from above, and comes down from the Father of lights, with whom there is no variation or shadow of turning." There is no good outside of God.

How can we discern in the difference between the messengers of a light and the Message of God's light? By knowing the Word of God. God's Holy Spirit and God's Word help us to identify right from wrong and good from evil. When we are full of the

---

[51] Exodus 7:10-12; 22; 8:7
[52] Galatians 1:6-9
[53] Matthew 24:11

truth, falsehood and spiritual deception are not difficult to recognize. When we are full of God's light, spiritual darkness is not hard to identify even though it have a wrapping of light. The spiritually dull and easily duped are those who walk in darkness for not spending time in light of God's Word. This is the reason God is calling His people back to read His Word. We live in perilous times, and they will only become increasingly difficult and spiritually confused. God needs His people to be solid and walking in the full light of His revealed truth. Read the Bible!

7
MAINTAINING THE LIGHT

Throughout his Gospel, the Apostle John refers to Jesus as the Word and the Light.

Just as God's Word spoke the Light into existence in the beginning, the same Word and the Light became incarnate in the man Jesus. The opening words to the Gospel of John remind us of the very beginning of creation: The same beginning of creation with God's Word and Light is creating a new beginning for humanity in Jesus Christ—who is God's Word and Light.

This same person, the Word of God in the flesh, who cried out "I am the Light of the world!" (John 8:12). God's Word brings life and light to humankind. In the utter chaos and darkness of a world steeped in sin, God sent the Light of the World, His own Son, Jesus Christ, to help us see life as God intended it to be. The good light of the good Creator illuminates things, not as we wish them to be, but as God created them to be. In the light of Jesus, we understand how God designed our lives to function. The theologian C.S. Lewis brilliantly observed, "I believe in Christianity as I believe that the sun has risen: not only because I see it, but because by it I see everything else."

THE OIL AND THE LAMP

Light is representative of God's presence. In the Tabernacle which God instructed Moses to build, one of the pieces of furniture was a lampstand which had seven little lamps upon it. Leviticus 24:1-4 describes the care that was to be given in tending the lamp of the Tabernacle: It was to be continually filled with oil so the light would not go out. There was never to be darkness in the sanctuary of the Lord, and the imagery is clear: We, as God's Temple, there is not to be any darkness in our hearts.

Light requires maintenance. If the flame of light does not have anything to burn, it will go out. Even in our days where flame lamps and candles are rarely used, even light bulbs need replacing and a constant flow of electricity. The priest was to tend the light and make sure it had the necessary fuel to burn brightly. Where there is no fuel, there is no sustaining light. Poor maintenance of God's light makes for a poor life with poor sight.

The lampstand of the Tabernacle also represents the Church. In the book of Revelation, Jesus commands the Apostle John to write to seven churches. In these seven churches were represented by seven lampstands (Revelation 1:20). In His correction to the church in Ephesus, Jesus says, "…repent and do the first works, or else I will come to you quickly and remove your lampstand from its place—unless you repent."

God has not made His Church to be a club, but a lighthouse and each individual part of His Church is to let God's light shine in and through it. Poor maintenance of the light also makes for a poor church. If a church—or a person—has no fuel for the Light inside them and the Light goes out, what good will they do in a dark world?

THE PARABLE OF THE OIL AND THE LAMPS
The maintenance of God's Light in our everyday life is paramount. Jesus illustrated this in a parable:

> Then the kingdom of heaven shall be likened to ten virgins who took their lamps and went out to meet the bridegroom. Now five of them were wise, and five were foolish. Those who were foolish took their lamps and took no oil with them, but the wise took oil in their vessels with their lamps. But while the bridegroom was

delayed, they all slumbered and slept. "And at midnight a cry was heard: 'Behold, the bridegroom is coming; go out to meet him!' Then all those virgins arose and trimmed their lamps. And the foolish said to the wise, 'Give us some of your oil, for our lamps are going out.' But the wise answered, saying, 'No, lest there should not be enough for us and you; but go rather to those who sell, and buy for yourselves.' And while they went to buy, the bridegroom came, and those who were ready went in with him to the wedding; and the door was shut. "Afterward the other virgins came also, saying, 'Lord, Lord, open to us!' But he answered and said, 'Assuredly, I say to you, I do not know you.' "Watch therefore, for you know neither the day nor the hour in which the Son of Man is coming. (Matthew 25:1-13)

Jesus is coming again—soon! His coming is the urgency for the call to repentance. Jesus requires a life of repentance from believers, not just non-believers. As we just saw in Revelation 2:5, in speaking to His Church, Jesus said that unless the churches repent of their sins, He will remove their light. This parable is a call to God's Church to tend the flame of God's presence with the oil, which throughout Scripture is indicative of the work of the Holy Spirit.

This is a scary parable. All ten of these virgins, these women who had been set apart and were waiting for the coming of the groom, were all in the same place, expecting the same person, anticipating the same result, with the same lamps which all had the same oil in them. The difference between half of them was the maintenance of the light, which is the supply of oil. Those whose oil had run dry missed out on everything.

It is possible to miss out on all that God is doing though we be part of the Church of Jesus Christ. We can be in the right place at the right time doing the right things but if our light has gone out, what then? There are people in our churches—people reading this book—who, without even realizing it, have allowed the supply of oil to run dry in their own personal lives.

Maintain the Flame

It was 3:30am on June 7, 2015 when the Lord woke me up. I tried to go back to sleep when I had the unmistakable impression that God was speaking to me. "Kyle, you are lazy!" He spoke to my heart. The words broke my heart because I knew they were true. I had become lazy in my prayer life and listening for God's voice. I had become especially lazy in reading my Bible. I got up and went downstairs and took a long time to repent before the Lord of my spiritual laziness. I prayed and read my

Bible for a long while.

It is easy to coast in our spiritual life because, well, it is easy. Pursuing the Lord, being filled, and being continually filled with the oil of God's Spirit, requires intentional diligence. It is much easier to be simply a nice person than it is to be an intentional, growing disciple of Jesus. Just as maintaining the flame of love in a marriage requires diligence, and raising godly children requires diligence, so does maintaining the flame of God's love and light in our personal lives. Hebrews 11:6 says, "He [God] is a rewarder of those who diligently seek Him." The reward is oil for our lamp so we will be ready for His coming—both the coming of what He wants to do in you and your church, and for the Second Coming of Christ Jesus. If this is you, God is calling you to repent lest He remove the unmaintained lampstand.

THE DARKNESS OF THE TIMES

One of the great issues facing the Church of our time is that of homosexuality and the agenda of the LGBTQ community. Not long ago, Bruce Jenner changed himself into a woman via surgery and hormones. All of us are aware that such perversions of the human body and image of God in a human being have been going on for decades, yet something was different with this instance. This time there was a sign that, if you were paying attention, you saw clearly. The sign was the cultural *response* to this man's intentional *de*formation, not his *trans*formation. This time, for the first time, there was a level of applause, veneration, adulation, and celebration from society that has not previously been seen. Furthermore, the Supreme Court of the United States just enacted a law redefining marriage to include homosexuality which has been met with great celebration across our country and world—and even in many sectors of the Church.

The issue is not homophobia as the cultural caricature of Christians fearing and hating people would have you believe. The issue it is light and dark. The prevailing thought of today's society is of absolute acceptance of any and every aberrant behavior, indeed we pushed rather forcibly to normalize anything people deem right in their own eyes. Those who adhere to the moral standards set by Someone higher than ourselves have now been deemed the abnormal ones. Those who follow God's laws and standards are bullied into submitting to the fashionable ways of thinking of society. Yet much of the Church falls into the trends of thinking that are contrary to God's Word. We, as human beings, think far too highly of what is currently cool or avant garde. My dad always told me, "Cool is overrated."

The flame is going out in many parts of the Church.

The oil has run out and darkness has crept into the Tabernacle of the Lord. It starts with faulty maintenance of the light—it starts with our own personal relationship with Jesus and our openness for the constant inflow of the Holy Spirit's life in our lives. It starts in the heart of God's people then it flows out to rest of the Church.

The prevailing darkness of the times is affecting the Church of Jesus Christ. Several denominations have accepted and blessed this deviation from God's Word. Many preachers who have come out in support of homosexual marriage have twisted God's Word to make it say what they want it—what is culturally PC to say instead of coming to the Scriptures to let God untwist the misperception. They do so under the cloak of being "relevant" to the culture. Being relevant is a means to an end, not the key to life. Relevance should be a fresh way of presenting the Gospel not changing the Gospel itself for cultural adulation.

Many have exchanged light for darkness. Our oil is drying up and our light is going out. The Church is beginning to believe and act like society. We have replaced our light with "relevance." It is also fascinating to note those who have the most ease in condoning sin are those who are most disconnected from the Church and God's Word. However, there are still many of people in the Church who remain pro-homosexual. Jesus warned His Church of the ever growing darkness and sinfulness of the times in Revelation 2:3-7:

> You have persevered and have patience, and have labored for My name's sake and have not become weary. Nevertheless I have this against you, that you have left your first love. Remember therefore from where you have fallen; repent and do the first works, or else I will come to you quickly and remove your lampstand from its place—unless you repent. But this you have, that you hate the deeds of the Nicolaitans, which I also hate. He who has an ear, let him hear what the Spirit says to the churches. To him who overcomes I will give to eat from the tree of life, which is in the midst of the Paradise of God.

The Nicolaitans is a symbolic group whose meaning in the Greek is "conquering the laity [people]." This was apparently a societal trend or group even within the Church that claimed a superior status and permitted idolatry and immorality.[54]

The key to the Church being all that Jesus designed us to be and to be in unity one with another is to walk in Jesus' light, not our preferred light. 1 John 1:7 teaches us, "But if we walk in the light as He is

---

[54] Spirit Filled Life Bible, commentary on Revelation 2:6

in the light, we have fellowship with one another, and the blood of Jesus Christ His Son cleanses us from all sin."

The light shows things for what they are, not how one would wish them to be. When electricity was introduced to individual homes around the turn of the 20th century, there are stories of people who saw how truly dirty their houses were for the first time. Since they had used the dim light of candles for so long, the soot and grime had built up. When the electric lights went on, they realized what dirtiness they had been living in.

The light of Jesus will show the ugliness inside of us if we will let it. We must move beyond being well-intentioned believers and come back to being diligent, intentional, and firmly-rooted believers who stand in the Light of the entire revelation of God's Word and not merely on a whimsical interpretation of it. God desires more than a *nice* Church, He wants a *pure* Church who lives in the light of His Word. He wants a Bride who is without "spot or wrinkle," (Ephesians 5:27) who is "washed with the water of His Word." For this reason "the time has come for judgment to begin at the house of God; and if it begins with us first, what will be the end of those who do not obey the gospel of God?" (1 Peter 4:17).

8
THE LIGHT OF SALVATION

I love my wife! She is a wonderful partner, mother, pastor, and woman of God. However, I did not grow to love her nor learn these things about her by simply observing her from afar, nor by just listening to her talk with other people. That is how I first noticed her, but falling in love is not done from afar. It is one thing to know about someone, and another thing entirely to *know* someone. I grew to love my wife because of the time I spent with her. I got to know her and she me. I did not win her over by doing things for her, but by showing her the caliber of man I am—and that comes through spending time getting to know one another. My wife is of such a high caliber, she actually didn't have to do too much to win me over!

Jesus said the same thing about our relationship to Him. In the day when we stand before Him to give account of our lives, He will say to many who have done wonderful things for Him, "I never *knew* you." Doing things for Jesus is not tantamount to knowing Him. Serving Him is not necessarily relating to Him.

The only ones who enter in to the fullness of Jesus' Kingdom's life and intimate relationship with Him are those who "do the will of My Father in Heaven."[55] Our salvation is not based on doing for God, it is based on faith, which in turn grows into intimate knowledge of God and obedience to Him. In other words, our doing for Jesus is not an end, it is a fruit; a result. Obedience is born out of love, not duty; it is born of close, intimate knowledge of God's heart, not robotic response to commands. The book of James has much more to say regarding the Word of God and salvation by way of obedience:

> "Therefore lay aside all filthiness and overflow of wickedness, and receive with meekness the implanted word, which is able to save your souls. But be doers of the word, and not hearers only, deceiving yourselves. For if anyone is a hearer of the word and not a doer, he is like a man observing his natural face in a mirror; for he observes himself, goes away, and

---

[55] Matthew 7:21-23

immediately forgets what kind of man he was. But he who looks into the perfect law of liberty and continues in it, and is not a forgetful hearer but a doer of the work, this one will be blessed in what he does."[56]

Though the vast majority of believers in Jesus Christ already have a Bible, many never make the habit of reading it with any sort of consistency. Many read a little bit every now and then, maybe a chapter every week….or month just to assuage the conscience of being neglectful this fundamental spiritual discipline. Perhaps church attendance, listening to the pastor's weekly sermon, or just listening to a sermon every now and again on TV or YouTube is what many would consider being "in the Word of God." Yet, as the Bible says of itself, how can God's Word instruct, train, or correct in righteous living[57] if we are not consistently learning from it through our spending time with Him?

A person who is growing in the Lord is not simply one who goes to Church, sings the worship songs, or prays. The primary method of growing in godliness has nothing to do with exterior veneers of religious piety and it has everything to do with knowing God's Word.

---

[56] James 1:21-25
[57] 2 Timothy 3:16

The Bible is living and active, and is able to penetrate and change our very being and transform us from the inside out.[58] It does not matter how many times we may have read the Bible. There are passages that I have either heard or read hundreds of times, if not thousands, yet there is something about the Holy Spirit-inspired, living Word of God that can bring new understanding and life from the same verse one has read over and over. This is because the Bible is much more than a book from Antiquity, it is written by inspiration of the Holy Spirit, and this same Holy Spirit lives in us. He brings the Bible alive and gives depth of meaning and understanding and new challenges regardless of how well we think we understand it.

THE GROWING WORD
James tells us to receive the "implanted Word" which is able to save our souls. It is interesting James says the Word of God saves our souls. Perhaps you are thinking, "I thought only Jesus can save us?" You are correct. But isn't Jesus also called the "Word of God"?[59] Jesus is the Word-made-flesh. Jesus is the revelation of God to us. Jesus is the perfection of our understanding of God in living flesh. It is through the Word that we are saved.

---

[58] Hebrews 4:12-13
[59] John 1:1-14

1 Peter 1:9 says, "the end of our faith is the salvation of our souls." The Word of God is able to show us salvation and keeps us in salvation. The final purpose of our faith in the death and resurrection of Jesus Christ, is our salvation. Do not misunderstand the purpose of our salvation. We are not saved to simply die and go to Heaven. The purpose of salvation is to save and restore the entire human being, every part. We were created in God's image and likeness[60], but His image in us was distorted due to sin's dominion over us. God desires so much more than our going to Heaven someday. He desires us to recover His perfect image in our whole person. God saved us to be transformed again into the image of God in Jesus Christ.[61] The implications of such a salvation are endless, but suffice it to say we cannot pigeon-hole the concept of salvation as simply "going to Heaven," rather it is the fullness of Heaven released in us and through us right here and now to transform us to be like Jesus and to touch the world around us with His love and power.

Since the end of our faith is our total salvation, then we must receive this "implanted Word" which is able to transform us into God's image. We come to

---

[60] Genesis 1:26
[61] Romans 8:29

faith through the Word of God,[62] and the Word of God was manifest through preaching.[63] Further, the unfolding, exposition, and teaching of the Word of God brings understanding to the simple.[64]

It is clear that through the Scriptures that God tells us He has **given** His Word, it is **preached**, and subsequently, His Word will **give light** and understanding. This means for us that 1) we need to spend time reading the Bible, and 2) go to church all the time to hear the exposition and teaching of the Word! As the Word of God is preached, the Holy Spirit is bringing light to people's hearts and changing them. This does not happen without studying the Bible or the action of the Holy Spirit. Both together form a powerful, life-changing combination!

Let's look for a moment at the phrase, "receive the *implanted* Word." The word implanted obviously refers to a seed that is sown into the heart of a person. Jesus likewise said in the Parable of the Sower that the Word of God is like a seed.[65] The seed was scattered upon the hard path, stony ground, ground filled with weeds, and finally, fertile ground.

---

[62] Romans 10:14-15
[63] Titus 1:3
[64] Psalm 119:30
[65] Luke 8:11-15

The seed that fell on the hard path was immediately snatched away by the birds and never took root. This symbolizes a hard heart and the Word of God is taken away by satan. The stony and weedy soils are people who received the Word of God with gladness. The seed took root and began to grow—but the hot sun scorched the newly sprouted plants in the stony soil because their roots did not go deep. Similarly, the weeds choked the life out of the Word because there was not sufficient room for it to grow. These things represent the hardships of life and the cares, worries, and desires of this life that disallow for the seed to grow to maturity. The only seed that produced fruit was that which fell in the good soil, and gave it sufficient room to take root and grow to ripeness.

If the Word is God is an implanted seed, it is alive. Jesus also likens our faith to a seed. Both God's Word and our faith are alive. What does one expect from a seed if not growth and ultimately fruit? If Jesus Himself says that God's Word is a living seed, then we should expect the same thing in our hearts—roots and fruits. The implanted Word in our hearts, as it begins to take root and germinate, begins to change everything about us. The heart is where the motives, worldview, and desires dwell, and the seed of the Word of God implanted in us will begin to produce a different kind of harvest in us: one that produces fruit that pleases God.

The garden of our hearts must be constantly tended. If we do not care for the seed, if we do not make room for it in our hearts, if we do not give it the right fertilizer, it will die inside of us. Not that this world is capable of changing God's Word or destroying it, but, as with everything living thing, it will die in the soil of our heart if we do not tend it. This was Jesus' point in the parable when He referred to the stony and weedy soils which disallowed room or health for growth.

It is easy to put reading God's Word and going to church on the back burner. After all, church will be there next week, and I can read the Bible whenever I want. But right now, I really have to work, or family is in town, or I am too tired…or whatever other excuse. When we attend to the distractions and difficulties of this life, we allow the implantation of the poisonous seeds of distractions, worldliness and ungodly attitudes to be planted and take root in our garden and the seed of God's Word soon becomes a dying, choked-out afterthought. God's Word will give an abundant harvest in our lives if we take care to work or cultivate our salvation to the point to fruitfulness.[66] This does not happen by accident—it is a constant, disciplined, and intentional process.

When I worked on the facilities staff at my church,

---

[66] Philippians 2:12

a certain day I had to go up on the roof of one of the buildings. On top of the building was the enormous air conditioning unit. As I looked at the unit, I noticed that there was a weed growing out of it! I was amazed that a seed was flown up by the wind, lodged in the A/C unit and, with what little moisture there was, it managed to sprout and grow. Weeds grow anywhere with little to no effort on our part. You will never see an apple tree or a tomato plant growing out of the A/C. These plants require abundant health to produce good fruit. Weeds require virtually nothing, and the nothingness they require produces a harvest of nothing in our lives in return.

It is the same with our own hearts. Weeds of all kinds naturally and easily grow in the sinful nature of our hearts. We don't even know how the seeds get there, but we are constantly bombarded by them. Yet to grow the good, healthy Fruit of the Spirit requires intentional cultivation and constant tending.

How, then, does the seed continue to grow in us to the point of harvest? By reading God's Word, hungering for it, and desiring and searching for it. Jesus said that if we search, we will find.[67] To the measure we search is the measure we will find. Perhaps you are thinking, "Pastor, I have tried all

---

[67] Matthew 7:7

this before, but I just don't understand the Bible." I am confident that the same Holy Spirit who wrote the Bible is the same Holy Spirit who lives in you. I am further confident that He is able to help you understand what is written. Before taking the Bible in your hands, ask Him for help and you will receive it. If there are still some issues understanding it, a practical help would be to switch the translation—use a more up to date version such as the New Living Translation, which is more modern English.

THE WORD IS A MIRROR

James continues his discourse on the Word of God by comparing it to a mirror. A mirror reflects our real condition, and it is by the light that we are able to see our reflection. When we wake up in the morning, the mirror does not hide the wrinkles, blemishes, bags under the eyes, or the wild bed-head. The mirror tells us exactly what we look like. The mirror does not try to show us what we want to see. It doesn't tell us what we look like by beating around the bush, it is the pinnacle of honesty. It reflects the real us, it is the opposite of photoshop!

So often we think we are just fine in the way we live our lives. It is easy to live the Instagram life because they only reflect back to us the things we like to see, but it is only the sinful, photoshopped version of ourselves which is reflected by a different light altogether.

Samuel Brengle, one of the founders of the Salvation Army, in his search to be more like Jesus, said, "I got my eyes off everybody but Jesus and myself, and I came to loathe myself." When all we do is compare ourselves with people we see around us, or to those we see as less than, we come out looking pretty good. When we compare ourselves to the standard of Jesus, we don't come out looking quite as nice!

It is easy to tap notes on a piano not knowing music thinking we are playing okay, but playing with skill and obeying the rules of music theory is another matter entirely. It is easy to think Cup-O-Noodles is a great meal when there is no knowledge of other, better foods. It is easy to live in the darkness and, by virtue of not being able to see, ignore the ugliness of sin in us. Similarly, it is easy to live according to our own conscience when we are unfamiliar with the rules of life God has set in place. But when we compare our lives to what is actually written in the truthful light and mirror of God's Word, and it reflects our actual condition back at us, we don't look nearly as good as we thought we did. As the Psalmist says,

> "Oh, that my actions would consistently reflect your decrees! Then I will not be ashamed when I compare my life with your commands."[68]

In other words, the psalmist is saying to the Lord, "fix me up, Lord, so that when I look in the mirror of your Word I look as wonderful as You!" The honest, truthful Word of God faithfully shows us where we are out of step with the character of God. God loves us so much that He sent His Word to discover our condition and recover His image in us. God's truthful love "is beautiful, but it is also terrible—terrible in its determination to allow nothing blemished or unworthy to remain in the beloved."[69]

Upon seeing ourselves as we really are, there is the need to respond to God's Word. James tells us to not only *hear* God's Word, but to *do it*. The person who does not put into practice the things pointed out to them in God's Word is like a person who sees himself in a mirror and promptly forget what he looks like. Let's examine for a moment this illustration of the mirror.

No one is at their best when they roll out of bed first thing in the morning. Our hair is wild. The remnants of drool and eye sleep are on our face. Our eyes are still blurry as we rub them. Our breath is horrid. The lines from our pillows still mark our faces. We are

---

[68] Psalm 119:5-6
[69] Hannah Hunnard. Hinds' Feet On High Places, 238

still in our pajamas. Then we hobble over to the bathroom and stand in front of the mirror—and it is a horrific scene. We shudder at the sight. All of a sudden, the phone rings and there is an emergency at work, and without hesitating or doing anything about our appearance, we dash out the door forgetting the appalling state in which we just saw ourselves. Of course, none of us would do that no matter how great the emergency. *<u>After seeing ourselves in the mirror, we immediately recognize our need for transformation</u>*—this is the ultimate point of the illustration!

When we compare our lives to what is written in God's Word, we see how woefully short we come to living it out—we see ourselves as we really are, which, is probably why people feel the need to twist it to fit their own personal ideologies instead of conforming themselves to it. God's Word helps us recognize our need to be continually transformed from the inside out. When we implement God's Word in our lives, we are changing the unkempt ugliness of our lives to look as beautiful as God is.

I remember when I was nineteen and twenty years old. Over those two years, my father sat down with me on a number of occasions to talk with me, and they were very difficult conversations. He was not angry, abusive, or denigrating. He was correcting and challenging his teenage son to mature. He would take hours to point out the areas of my life where I was legitimately deficient. He held nothing back, though he said it with love. The Bible tells us to speak the truth with love. I once heard a pastor say, "Truth without love is brutality. Love without truth is hypocrisy. Truth with love is growth." Every word my father spoke to me was like a dagger in the chest because his observations about my life were accurate—and I knew it. I remember thinking in one specific moment it was as if he was holding a mirror in front of me and showing me who I really was because I had not the maturity to see it on my own.

During one particular five-hours-long conversation, the thought crossed my mind, "I have a choice to make: either the old man is crazy and I will go on living my life as I desire, or I will accept correction from a man who loves me and is far wiser than I." I consciously decided the latter. These conversations with my father were a turning point in my life, they took me from adolescence to manhood. God's Word is the same—it tells us like it is. God does not want us to miss any of the blessings He has for us, but such blessings are obtained exclusively by living according to His Word. His Word shows us who we really are and what God requires of us. Now the decision is ours to accept or reject the truthful mirror of His Word.

We need to decide when we read something convicting or something that drives deep down into our souls, we are going to be people who say, "Lord, change me into Your image according to Your Word." We must be people who say, "Thy will be done!" not, "My will be done!"

One thing I have said to my children ever since they were little babies is "ears to hear, and hearts to obey" as a life-long theme of growing in Jesus. It is difficult to live this way, but no one said life in Jesus would be easy, either. Transformation into God's image is not a simple or painless process.

At the end of James' short discourse on the implanted Word, he says this…listen closely,

> But he who looks into the perfect law of liberty and continues in it, and is not a forgetful hearer but a doer of the work, this one will be blessed in what he does. If anyone among you thinks he is religious, and does not bridle his tongue but deceives his own heart, this one's religion is useless. Pure and undefiled religion before God and the Father is this: to visit orphans and widows in their trouble, and to keep oneself unspotted from the world.[70]

Why does James put the exhortation of: 1) guard you tongue, 2) help people, and 3) keep yourself

---

[70] James 1:25-27

pure, in the same place along with the concept of God's Word reflecting who we are as people? It is because "pure religion" is found in doing good. Doing good is the outward demonstration of what God has "implanted" in our hearts through His Word—this "pure religion" of loving people and keeping ourselves pure is the power of the Word living through us! Good works naturally happen when the implanted Word begins to grow in us to produce good fruits. We do not live basing our faith or identity upon our actions, rather, when God's Word begins to grow in us, our actions will accurately reflect the goodness of God's Word. That is what seed does: it reproduces its own kind, therefore, the seed of God's Word should produce the fruits of God's Word in us.

If we are not reading God's Word, we run the risk of our faith dying for lack of fuel. The Apostle Paul wrote to the church in Philippi about guarding their faith from those who would destroy it saying, "I never get tired of telling you these things, and I do it to safeguard your faith."[71] God's Word both shows us the way of salvation, and living out His Word keeps us safely in it. "How can a young man cleanse his way? By taking heed according to Your Word."[72]

---

[71] Philippians 3:1 (NLT)
[72] Psalm 119:9

LIVING GOD'S WORD

We need to remember that everything James wrote in his letter is inextricably linked to the concepts he has already introduced and we have been discussing already: 1) pure religion (or another way of saying this is "the kind of living that pleases God") is to keep yourself unsoiled from sin and serve others, especially those who are in need (1:27), and 2) fulfilling the "Royal Law" or the "Law of Liberty" by which we will be judged. This law simply states: "Love your neighbor as yourself," (2:8-12). The entire book of James develops these two concepts. Most everything in the book of James runs through the lens of purity of living and serving others. James 2:14-20 continues the development of the concept of the mirror into some very practical applications:

> What does it profit, my brethren, if someone says he has faith but does not have works? Can faith save him? If a brother or sister is naked and destitute of daily food, and one of you says to them, "Depart in peace, be warmed and filled," but you do not give them the things which are needed for the body, what does it profit? Thus also faith by itself, if it does not have works, is dead. But someone will say, "You have faith, and I have works." Show me your faith without your works, and I will show you my faith by my works. You believe that there is one God. You do well. Even the demons

believe—and tremble! But do you want to know, O foolish man, that faith without works is dead?

In light of his discussion on the merit of our good works, James posits the question, "Can faith save…?" The insinuation is faith alone does not save. This would seem to be a contradictory concept to everything we understand of salvation. Of course faith can save—it's the only thing that does! It is only God's grace through faith that we have salvation. Nothing else can suffice or substitute. The Apostle Paul says salvation is not by works,[73] and now James tells us it is through works. What is the difference?

In a very practical way, James explains what he means. What good is it to say we have faith and then not serve another person, especially one in need? If someone is cold or hungry, saying, "God bless you" is not going to clothe or feed them. We would be cold-hearted people if someone were dying right in front of us and it is within our power to feed them but all we do is quote a Bible verse. This is not even close to the heart and character of God. The Apostle Paul speaks of faith as being what takes us out of a life of sin through the death and resurrection of Jesus Christ. James speaks of stimulating this same saving faith toward serving

---

[73] Ephesians 2:8-9

people so it does not become something selfish or apathetic. Paul speaks of faith *__making us right with God__*, James speaks of this same faith as living through us to *__be like God__* in the way we conduct our lives.

THE FRUIT OF THE SEED

A principle of both physical and spiritual life is each seed reproduces after its own kind. This rule of life carries consequences both for good and bad: we reap what we sow.[74] The implanted Word is a seed, and this seed must bear fruit in the life of the disciple. It is simply what seeds do: they multiply life and produce more fruit. In fact, Jesus specifically told us in John 15:16 that we are called by Him to bear fruit and that our fruit should remain.

So what does this fruit look like? James has already told us—it looks like "pure religion." It is, at it's core, the "law of liberty" of loving your neighbor as yourself. Consequently, this "law of liberty," as James puts it, is what precisely the Scripture Jesus said the _entirety_ of the revealed Word of God hangs on.[75] Did you hear that? The fullness of God's revealed Word—the character of God Himself—the essence of the fruit that the Word of God produces in us comes down to this: Love God with

---

[74] Galatians 6:7-8; Genesis 1:11
[75] Matthew 22:40

everything you've got, and love others as you love yourself.[76]

James has very clear in his mind the kind of faith that saves: it is the "implanted Word" which is able to save. After we repent of our sins and receive God's salvation through Jesus Christ, the Word of God in us and living through us is actual evidence of this faith transforming us. This type of faith has to be in a certain form and James is describing exactly what God is looking for in our lives that would be evidence of this fruit-bearing seed. It is loving God and loving others, but James describes this fruit of our faith in our everyday lives: 1) stop living in sin, (1:27), 2) do not play favorites with people, (2:3-4), 3) love your neighbor and serve others, (2:8-12), 4) tame the tongue because a loose and unbridled tongue makes for a defiled person, (3:6).

Great ministry, religious rituals, acts of devotion, fasting, and evangelism are not the fruit God primarily looks at. The fruit that most pleases Him is love, and the manifest form of love should be in care and genuine, heart-felt service to others. If love is not the central component of the fruit, then all our knowledge, sacrifice, faith, and ministry has been in vain.[77] Further, the only specific definition of

---

[76] Matthew 22:35-40
[77] 1 Corinthians 13:1-3

"fruit" we are given in the Bible is, "love, joy, peace, patience, kindness, goodness, faithfulness, gentleness, and self-control."[78] These character traits, known as the Fruit of the Spirit, are the precise description of God's own character. The fruitfulness of our lives God mainly looks for is if we are bearing the same character traits He has. But it is also God's will that our fruit should remain.[79] Consider what 2 Peter 1:3-8 gives as a definition for remaining fruitful:

> ...as His divine power has given to us all things that pertain to life and godliness, through the knowledge of Him who called us by glory and virtue, by which have been given to us exceedingly great and precious promises, that through these you may be partakers of the divine nature, having escaped the corruption that is in the world through lust. But also for this very reason, giving all diligence, add to your faith virtue, to virtue knowledge, to knowledge self-control, to self-control perseverance, to perseverance godliness, to godliness brotherly kindness, and to brotherly kindness love. For if these things are yours and abound, you will be neither barren nor unfruitful in the knowledge of our Lord Jesus Christ.

---

[78] Galatians 5:22-23
[79] John 13:14

If God's Word is a seed, then the fruit of that seed should be according to its own kind. The fruit of the implanted Word is our living out the Word itself in every aspect of our lives, it is the Word-in-flesh—*our flesh!* We are crucified with Christ and we no longer live, but Christ, the Word Incarnate, lives incarnated in us.[80] Therefore, Jesus is making *us* the Word incarnate to every person in the world around us. If we do not love or serve them; if we allow ourselves to continue to be contaminated by sin; if we love position, money, authority, and pride more than we love people, then the Word of God does not dwell in us, and our fruit is bad.

If Jesus comes to find fruit in our lives and He finds ministry with no love, big church without the character of Jesus, nice deeds with no internal transformation, or ministry with one's self as the primary motivation, this fruitlessness will be cut down.[81] ***Jesus is looking for people whose fruit looks like Him.***

1 Corinthians 13:1-3

If I speak in the tongues of men and of angles, but have not love, ***I AM A NOISY GONG OR A CLANGING CYMBAL.***
(even exhibiting the gifts of the Spirit, without the

---

[80] Galatians 2:20
[81] Luke 13:6-9; John 15:1-5

fruit of love I become annoying to God for my pretentious displays of religiosity).

And if I have prophetic powers, and understand all mysteries and all knowledge, and if I have all faith, so as to remove mountains, but have not love, ***I AM NOTHING.***
(Even with great teaching ability and powerful ministry, without the fruit of love I am not pleasing to God).

If I give away all I have, and if I deliver up my body to be burned, but have not love, ***I GAIN NOTHING.***
(all my strength, ministry, sacrifice, and piety without the fruit of love were all in vain, and my reward from God is in jeopardy).

9
TRAINING IN THE LIGHT

When I was in high school, I was a good athlete. I played basketball and ran track. I could slam-dunk a basketball touching the rim almost with my elbow. I could clear 6'4" in the high jump and my team broke our school record in the 4 x100 relay race. Two decades later, the story is somewhat different. I have not been very involved in sports since then. I am not in as good a shape I was when I was 17 and 18, I weigh more than I did then, and my muscles are not as strong, therefore, I cannot do the same things I did in high school. I also happen to remember my dad telling me that one of the first things to go is the knees. He was right! They just aren't as springy as they once were. If I were to get myself back into the same shape I was twenty years ago, it would require an amazing amount of diligence and intentionality. It would not be accidental nor simply a nice idea. There would need to be a change about every part of my life—my diet and exercise would be the primary changes needed among some other things. As all of us are acutely aware, such changes are quite difficult. They are not whimsical, accidental, or unplanned, they require discipline and training.

For I while I used to teach Spanish. I saw one of my students about three years after she finished my course. I told her that I was pastoring a Spanish-speaking church and invited her to come. She was happy for the invitation, but she kindly told me that she did not remember anything from my course. That made me feel just wonderful as a professor! The simple fact is that she had not practiced for those three years. You either use it or lose it. One is either advancing or going backwards—there is no happy middle ground.

Unfortunately, it is easier to get fat than to stay fit. It is easier to stay in your comfortable language than to force yourself to continue to grow in another. It is easier to destroy than to build. It is easier to grow weeds than fruit. It is easier to live in sin than in righteousness. It is easier to curse than to bless. It is easier to lose than to win. It is easier to argue than to make peace. It is easier to give in than to resist. It is easier to wear the veneer of religion than to have a growing relationship with Jesus. In athletics, life, academics, and spiritual living, (body, soul, and spirit) there is no such thing as stagnation—if you are not moving forward, you are falling back.

In several places the Bible compares our spiritual lives to athletic competition. As with any competition, no one competes to lose. No one likes to lose. We hear things all the time about sports not mattering if you win or lose, but how you play the game. I am all for good sportsmanship and bettering one's self—but who are they kidding? We like to win. Winning feels good, losing does not.

When our spiritual life is on the line, God wants us to win. We are called "more than conquerors in Christ Jesus,"[82] and that is not the talk nor expectation of a loser. The Apostle Paul tells us, "Don't you realize that in a race everyone runs, but only one person gets the prize? So run to win!"[83] We are instructed to win—and God has given us two things that will ensure our victory and, along with the victory, the prize that comes with it: 1) the power of His Holy Spirit working us to give us the strength to run this race, and 2) His Word, which gives us the instructions on how the race is to be won.

---

[82] Romans 8:37
[83] 1 Corinthians 9:24 (New Living Translation)

Since we have both the grace of God by His Holy Spirit and the Word of God as our instruction, we are prepared to win. However, this race is fraught with danger and obstacles that threaten to take us out. These obstacles are sin and demonic interference.

> Therefore we also, since we are surrounded by so great a cloud of witnesses, let us lay aside every weight, and the sin which so easily ensnares us, and let us run with endurance the race that is set before us, looking unto Jesus, the author and finisher of our faith."
> (Hebrews 12:1-2)

Looking unto Jesus is the only way to win. When all is said and done, you and I are unable to win or even stay the course. "But those who wait on the Lord shall renew their strength; they shall mount up with wings like eagles, they shall run and not be weary, they shall walk and not faint."[84]

DILIGENCE IN TRAINING

Since nothing happens by accident, and we are either advancing or sliding backwards in our abilities physically, mentally, or spiritually, and we are in this spiritual race to win and not lose, listen to the hard words that the author of the book of Hebrews has for his readers:

---

[84] Isaiah 40:31

> [Jesus Christ was] called by God as High Priest "according to the order of Melchizedek," of whom we have much to say, and hard to explain, since **you have become dull** of hearing. For though by this time you ought to be teachers, **you need someone to teach you again** the first principles of the oracles of God; and **you have come to need milk** and not solid food. For everyone who partakes only of milk is unskilled in the word of righteousness, for he is a babe. But solid food belongs to those who are of full age, that is, those who by reason of use have their senses exercised [trained!] to discern both good and evil.[85]

The readers are being excoriated by their teacher. Three times he mentions their regress. They have *become* dull, they are in need to teaching *again*, and they have *come to need milk* instead of solid food. This means that before this point, they were *not* dull, *skilled* in the Word of God, and able to have *solid food*—but they are no longer this way. They had not advanced in the Word of God or their spiritual life, nor had they stagnated—they had slipped backwards. They were spiritual adults, and now they have fallen back to being spiritual babies.

The author of Hebrews reproaches his people because he needs to go over the fundamentals they

---

[85] Hebrews 5:10-14 (italics mine)

had forgotten, and it had gotten to the point that he was unable to advance and tell them the other things he desired to teach because of inability to understand. Whereas Paul had told Timothy to train himself to be godly,[86] which, of course requires constant diligence, these people had slipped into a life of complacency and religiosity, causing spiritual dullness.

There is always the need to advance in what God has given to us. There is always more to grow, more to learn, and more to understand of God. Jesus said as much to His disciples:

> I still have many things to say to you, but you cannot bear them now. However, when He, the Spirit of truth, has come, He will guide you into all truth; for He will not speak on His own authority, but whatever He hears He will speak; and He will tell you things to come.[87]

Though Jesus was not reprimanding His disciples for falling backwards, He was insisting that, even though they had already spent three years with Him, there was much more room to grow in their understanding of Himself and of spiritual things. It does not matter how much we know or for how long we have walked with Jesus—if God is so great and

---

[86] 1 Timothy 4:7 (New Living Translation)
[87] John 16:12-13

unlimited in His wisdom and power, then there will never be a moment where we do not need more of Him and cannot learn more of Him.

If athletes desire to compete in the Olympic games, they must wait for them to come around. Since the games come every four years, there is nothing to be done to hurry their arrival, but there is much to be done in the meantime. The athletes are not wasting time watching TV, eating hamburgers and ice cream. They train hard. They are focused, disciplined, and intentional in everything they do so they are prepared for when the moment of competition comes.

After so much diligent training, the athlete wins the gold medal at the Olympic games. Yet it would be foolish to throw in the towel and stop training, especially if he or she has good years of competition left. Just because he or she won a gold medal, and for one fleeting moment is the best in the world, this does not by any means guarantee the top spot for life! In order to stay there, he or she must continue to advance, train, and be diligent.

It is equally as dangerous to be a mature believer in Jesus Christ who thinks he knows everything, as it is for a new believer who does not know much. The mature believers are at risk of slipping backwards by coming to the place of complacency and so much "knowledge" they no longer feel the need to continue in the same diligence in which they once lived. The young believers are particularly susceptible to traps, wrecked faith, and other things that derail or interfere with life in Jesus.

There exists a mentality of entitlement or of self-satisfaction or self-righteousness that can subtly creep into the believers' lives when they have gone to church all their lives, or reached a certain "level" at church such as deacon, elder, pastor, group leader, etc. There is the smugness of believing "I have arrived with God" and I can just coast for the rest of my life. Be careful. That is dangerous.

When we do not use our physical muscles, they atrophy. It does not matter how strong or how athletic we once were, if we do not use our muscles, we will begin to lose them. When we are driving, the moment we lift our foot from the accelerator, and we begin to coast, we are no longer driving forward, we are slowly coming to a stop. Our spiritual lives are no different. They will atrophy the moment we being to relax, and they will slowly come to a stop the moment we stop accelerating.

SLIPPING BACKWARDS
When the author of Hebrews upbraids his listeners for their backsliding, he is speaking to the tendencies of every one of us. The context of Hebrews 5 gives us greater understanding to what

he is referring. In the preceding verses, he is talking about Jesus being of the priesthood in the line of Melchizedek and not of Aaron. (If you happen to have no idea of what any of that means, then you need to continue to grow in your understanding of Jesus. Read and study your Bible! ☺). The author is telling his readers that he needs to go back to re-teach them about who Jesus Christ is when they had already known before.

The context also tells us they had fallen backwards and they were actually leaving the grace of Christ's salvation to go back to depending on the Law in order to become right with God. The title of this biblical book is "Hebrews," so the readers are Hebrews—Jews—Israelites. They were leaving the liberty of Christ to return to the dead works of the flesh in trying to win salvation by obeying the Law, and the author is telling them *again* who Jesus is. Yet this is the tendency of each one of us.

FALLING BACK INTO WORKS
The tendency in the mentality of every believer is to receive the grace of Christ Jesus with gladness—but then we slip into the mentality of believing that either we do not deserve such amazing grace when we remember the past, or we become so careless with God's grace we slip back into easy sin. The liberty of Jesus is slowly replaced with the religiosity of working for our salvation or the faulty

way of thinking that it is easier to get forgiveness than permission thereby relegating God's grace to a cheap favor. We may not even admit it to ourselves, or consciously think it, but I have been a pastor too long and have known too many people who begin to live out of a sense of working, not to earn salvation, but to feel like they are worthy and deserving of God's great love for them. In so doing, they forget the whole point of Jesus' life: God loved us even when we were sinners and sent Jesus to pay the price for our sins to restore relationship with Him. None of that depends on our works either before or after salvation.

We read the Bible more, go to church more, worship harder, and fast longer. None of those things are bad—please do them! But the subtle, even unperceived mentality, is if we do more, then God must love us more. The reality is there is nothing we have done, are doing, or will do, which will serve as motivation for God to love us more than He already does. God's love, blessings, promises, eternal life, inheritance, and forgiveness, are through Christ Jesus and His death and resurrection, not through our trying harder.

When we begin to live by slipping back into good works as motive for God's love and salvation, all those "good things" become chores. I have seen many people working hard in the ministry with the semblance of godliness and goodness, and after a short time of shining brightly and burning hotly for the Lord, they burn out and you don't see them again. Why? Because they had fallen back into "doing" for the Lord to earn His favor and love, it was a "must do" that they hoped would bring about transformation.

Our outward works do not produce inward change, instead it is the inward change of the Holy Spirit that gives definition and value to the works we do. It is the work of the Holy Spirit that keeps our lamps filled with oil and the flame of love burning brightly during our whole lives. When this is the case, work for the Lord is not a chore, it is born out of our hearts because of our great love for Him. Our doing needs to spring from our being—from the person God is making us to be. "Doing" does not transform our lives. A transformed life finds itself "doing" good things!

We are no longer slaves to the fear that if we do not do something for God then we will fall out of His favor. Rather we serve Him because we are so firm in His promises, love, and goodness that we never tire. It is by His grace we are saved. It is also by His grace that we are sustained for our whole lives to run the whole race until the end. Those who wait upon the Lord will run and not faint.[88]

---

[88] Isaiah 40:31

10
MEDITATING IN THE LIGHT

A LOST ART
There is a lost art of walking in the light in present day Christianity. Of course walking in the light as Jesus is in the light requires purity of living, but in order to do so, we must be filled with God's Word, which will give us His light. Jesus is both the Light of the World and the Word of God—if we are filled with His Word, we are filled with His Light.

The lost art I am referring to is meditating on God's Word. This is not merely reading God's Word. This is not simply listening to a sermon. This is an intentional, passionate pursuit to know God and understanding His character through deep thinking and study of His Word. This is not as hard as it sounds, but it does require discipline. This discipline will lead to a life of deepened faith, because faith comes by hearing, and hearing by the Word of God.[89]

Meditating on God's word and being still and quiet before the Lord, "being still and knowing the He is God" is essential for learning to live and walk in the light. Christians get scared of the word "meditation," but the Bible is replete with this concept. I am not talking about eastern meditation practiced by Buddhists or Hindus, this is a form of meditation that seeks contact with the dark spiritual world. This is meditating in and on the Light of God's Word. Learning to be still and quiet yourself down in order to wait upon the Lord is the focusing of your spirit and connecting with God, His Spirit and His Word on a deeper level which will provoke great intimacy with Him and great transformation in our lives.

KNOWLEDGE AND REVELATION

Meditating on God's Word will lead to a life filled with revelation. There is an enormous difference between knowledge and revelation. Ephesians 1:17 tells us that our ability to grow in our spiritual understanding of God comes from the "spirit of wisdom and revelation." Head-knowledge does not change our lives. Information is not tantamount to transformation.

---

[89] Romans 10:17

I was once introduced to man who was touted by his friend as a great teacher of God's Word with incredible knowledge. I met the man and it turned out he lived under a bridge, and several weeks later we had to ask him to not come back to the church because he was threatening people with physical violence. This was not a man whose life was changed at all and not living at all as a follower of Jesus should. It did not matter how much he knew about God's Word—he was not living in the light. He had some head knowledge, but that obviously did not transform his life, nor had he fully given himself to what he supposedly had learned. If we seek, we will find—but when we find, we must give ourselves completely to it, then the revealed, uncovered, demystified Word of God will penetrate our hearts and begin to take root and transform our lives.

Wisdom and revelation that come from the Spirit of God, however, shine His light in our inner person and bring deep, life-changing understanding. We could read the Bible 1,000 times, and still receive new revelation from it. His Word is alive and full of light, and if we will dedicate ourselves to it, we too will be filled with His light.

CONNECTING ON A SPIRITUAL LEVEL
Meditating on God's Word is not a mental exercise.

Though we do implement our mind, our mind cannot receive things directly from the Spirit of God. In John 4:24, Jesus said, "God is Spirit and those who worship Him must worship in spirit and in truth." Since God is Spirit, and we too are spiritual beings, then we must learn to connect with Him via our spirit. It would then be right to say that God is Spirit, and those who *worship, commune, talk, pray, love, share, know, and connect* with God must do so through the spirit He has put into us. Our spirits were designed to connect with His Spirit. Listen to the Apostle Paul says regarding this same subject:

> …no one knows the things of God except the Spirit of God. Now we have received, not the spirit of the world, but the Spirit who is from God, that we might know the things that have been freely given to us by God…the natural man does not receive the things of the Spirit of God, for they are foolishness to him; nor can he know them, because they are spiritually discerned. [90]

Psalm 46:10 says simply, "Be still and know that I am God." Meditating on God's Word, hearing from His Spirit, and learning to be still and quiet before the Lord is where we begin to access God's Spirit,

---

[90] 1 Corinthians 2:11b-12, 14

the riches of His Word, His voice, His instruction, and His understanding at a different level. When we are quiet and meditating on God and His Word, He will begin to reveal to us things which transcend our limited, human understanding. We begin to connect with God's Word, as Paul prayed for the Ephesians, with the "spirit of wisdom and revelation." This is never to be misunderstood as revelation that is contrary to God's Word or His established norms, however, the spirit of wisdom and revelation may frequently fly in the face of established norms cherished by man but not necessarily established by God.

Learning to be still and quiet ourselves down in order to wait upon the Lord is really the focusing of our spirit. Have you ever been so focused on something that you were in capable of hearing, paying attention to, or even noticing anything else around you? Men are very good at that. When we are interested in what's on the TV, we cannot hear what our wives are saying! It is the same thing in walking in the spirit, meditating on God's word, and calming your soul in order to focus on God. Our focus is so strong on God that we do not notice anything else around us, because we are so focused, tuned in, and intent on him.

This takes practice. We live in a culture where there is very little quietness or introspection. There is constant bombardment with noise. We have grown so accustomed to it we hardly notice it anymore. Just try silence for a few minutes. Go to a place where there is no visual or auditory stimuli. If we are unaccustomed to it, we will find the mind doesn't quite know what to do. Just as an excited puppy needs to be trained to walk next to its master, so our minds can be trained to be quiet, submitted, and not wandering. But it is precisely in these spiritual disciplines of solitude and silence where we begin to encounter God at another level. As we train our bodies, so can we train our minds and spirits to focus on God both His Word, and His Spirit. Isn't part of the Fruit of the Spirit "self-control"? We can control our **ENTIRE** being: body, soul, and spirit. When we do this, God's Word will begin to come alive to us in fresh and powerful ways.

FILL UP THE SPIRITUAL TANK

Psalm 12:6 says, "The words of the LORD are pure words, like silver tried in a furnace…purified seven times." God's Word is refined and ready for our consumption. Think of it this way: God's Word is like refined gasoline which we need to live, function, and have good success in our relationship with Him. If your car needed to be filled with gas, you would not open up the hood and dump gasoline directly on the motor. Why? Because the motor *cannot* receive it that way. You need to put the gas in the tank and the fuel injector pumps it into the internal parts of the engine where it is usable. The spirit is the gas tank and fuel injector, and the mind/soul is the engine. The Word of God is considered foolishness by those who try to connect with it through the feebleness of the human mind. But when we connect with it by the spirit through listening to the Spirit of God, the spirit then pumps it into our minds and that is the moment when we "get it."

THREE LEADERS
There are three amazing leaders of Israel who deeply meditated on God's Word and left us detailed instructions on how to do it. God, through Moses, Joshua, and David, show us how His Word will lead to a great reward: We will be fruitful, prosperous, and have His life in us.[91]

MOSES: LEST WE FORGET
The book of Deuteronomy is Moses' final address to the people of Israel before his death and their entrance into the Promised Land. Deuteronomy 6:1-12 is a rather long passage, but absolutely necessary to our understanding of the value of the art and discipline of meditating on God's Word. I will break it up into more bite-sized portions and we will look at it more closely.

---

[91] Deuteronomy 6:2-3; Joshua 1:7; Psalm 1:2-3

"Now this is the commandment, and these are the statutes and judgments which the LORD your God has commanded to teach you, that you may observe them in the land which you are crossing over to possess, that you may fear the LORD your God, to keep all His statutes and His commandments which I command you, you and your son and your grandson, all the days of your life, and that your days may be prolonged. Therefore hear, O Israel, and be careful to observe it, that it may be well with you, and that you may multiply greatly as the LORD God of your fathers has promised you—'a land flowing with milk and honey.'" (6:1-3)

The "Promised Land" that we are possessing is our new life in Christ Jesus. More specifically, it is "every spiritual blessing in the heavenly realms."[92] We are new creations in Jesus Christ and we are to possess ***everything*** of Heaven, and bring Heaven onto earth, live in Heaven's fullness of life, power, authority, and glory as mature sons and daughters of God. Israel itself and the blessings of the Promised Land they were to inherit were but a shadow of who we are in Jesus and what we are to possess in the spiritual realms. But, as it was with Israel, so it is with us—obtaining and living in all these enormous

---

[92] Ephesians 1:3 (NLT)

blessings is predicated on the observance of and commitment to the Word of God.

> "Hear, O Israel: The LORD our God, the LORD is one! You shall love the LORD your God with all your heart, with all your soul, and with all your strength. And these words which I command you today shall be in your heart. (6:4-6)

God is first and His Word has preeminence in our lives. When God is first, we have revelation of the height, width, depth, and length of His amazing love. Putting and keeping God first provokes in us a deeper love and desire for His presence and Word.

Jesus said that where our treasure is, there our hearts will also be.[93] If you are having a difficult time connecting with God, reading His Word, or you feel that your first love for God has grown cold, it is a sure thing that God is no longer first in your life—other things have risen to take His place and have stolen your passion redirecting them to other things or people in your life. Where, what, and whom is your treasure?

> You shall teach them diligently to your children, and shall talk of them when you sit in your house, when you walk by the way, when you lie down, and when you rise up. (6:7)

---

[93] Matthew 6:21

The Hebrew word used here for "teach" is "shanan," and it means to whet/sharpen or pierce/wound. It is the imagery of a sword that is both sharpened and quick to pierce; a sword ready for battle. Such is the teaching and power of God's Word.

Both Ephesians 6:17 and Hebrews 4:12 tells us that the Word of God is a Sword. In Ephesians, the "Word" is the Greek word "rhema" which is a word of *revelation*. In Hebrews, the "Word" is the Greek word "logos" which refers to the *written* Word of God. When we read God's Word with the spirit of revelation, we have a double-edged sword of both the written and revealed Word (which is God's Word for a specific moment for wisdom and instruction) that is instructive, corrective, and is able to sharpen and train us for all godliness and lead us out of danger.

This Sword needs to be ready at any moment to guide our own persons and instruct our families. There was a time when my wife and I found a series of shows on Netflix which we enjoyed. The show was interesting, funny, and wholesome. One day as we watched the show with our children, at the end of this particular episode, there was a strong theme of homosexuality. At the end of the show (which since that moment we stopped watching the series), Teresa and I sat down with our kids, opened up

God's Word and instructed them for quite a while on what the Bible says regarding homosexuality—particularly from Romans 1:18-32.

That is what this verse is saying when it says to talk of God's Word when you are sitting in your home, walking down the road, going to bed, and getting up in the morning. The teaching of God's Word in any moment is a sharp sword that will cut through the lies that swirl around us and our children. When the teaching and meditation on God's word is a daily, we are "redeeming the time" looking for God's righteousness, truth, and goodness in every moment.

The revelation of God's Word through diligent talking about it and studying of it, will change everything about our lives. The Sword of God's Word will pierce us to cut out sin and will sharpen us so we are spiritually alive and ready.

> You shall bind them as a sign on your hand, and they shall be as frontlets between your eyes. (6:8)

Everything about our actions (*hand*) and our thoughts (*between your eyes*) need to be directed by God's Word and filled with His Light—this is walking in the light and the renewing of our minds so we may have the mind of Christ Jesus. Psalm 19:14 says, "Let the words of my ***mouth*** and the meditation of my *heart* be acceptable in Your sight…" The things we think about (meditate on) and that to which we set our hands needs to be in the light so we will not sin in either thought or action.

> You shall write them on the doorposts of your house and on your gates. (6:9)

Etching them on the doors of our house is a reminder that this house serves the Lord. But our own bodies and hearts are a temple for the Holy Spirit, too. God's Word is to be carved, written, and etched on our hearts—it is to be part of us. Proverbs 7:3 says to write God's Word "on the tablet of your heart." God Himself also says in Jeremiah 31:33, "…I will put My law in their minds, and write it on their hearts; and I will be their God, and they shall be My people."

In Ezekiel 8:6-11, God gave Ezekiel a vision of the Temple where the leaders of Israel were in a dark, hidden room about which no one knew. They were there worshipping the images of idols and all kinds of unclean things which were carved into walls of this secret room deep in God's Temple where no one would see them. They thought they could live a double life of worshipping their heart's desires of the unclean things of the culture around them while still appearing religious and pious to everyone around them.

We must be careful with the things we choose to set before us—what websites we frequent, what Netflix shows we browse, whose Instagram we chose to follow and browse, and what music we listen to, etc.—all of those things etch themselves on to the walls of our Temple. Things that we frequent and give our time and worship to, the things nobody sees or knows about, yet they still contaminate our Temple. We must be careful to live in the Light because God will judge every part of our lives—even the secret places no one else sees.[94] If you have been hiding things deep in your heart that do not please God, repent and He will forgive you. This is why we are to meditate on God's Word: it is pure and keeps us clean.

"So it shall be, when the LORD your God brings you into the land of which He swore to your fathers, to Abraham, Isaac, and Jacob, to give you large and beautiful cities which you did not build, houses full of all good things, which you did not fill, hewn-out wells which you did not dig, vineyards and olive trees which you did not plant—when you have eaten and are full— then beware, ***lest you forget*** the LORD who brought you out of the land of Egypt, from the house of bondage."[95] (6:10-12)

---

[94] Romans 2:16; Ecclesiastes 12:14

Moses is speaking of a time when Israel would fully occupy the Promised Land and be satisfied with its abundance. Up to this point, the entire discourse has been about adherence to God's Word and keeping Him first in everything. Yet Moses foresaw the challenge that awaited Israel, as this same challenge confronts all of us: that they [we] would forget the Lord. Because of the abundance of the land, Moses feared they would slowly push God farther and farther down on their priority list, and their love would eventually be transferred from God to their abundance. Once God is no longer the priority, then neither is His character manifesting in and through our lives.

Moses' caution was to ***always*** keep our hearts, minds, and affections set on the Lord regardless of the season we are in, whether it is poor or prosperous; joyful or sad; easy or challenging. We must do this lest we forget the Lord. If we are feasting on God's Word, filled with its light, and letting it engrave itself deeply into our entire being, then we will never forget and thus, always possess the land with great prosperity, abundance, and life.

JOSHUA: STEWARDING THE LIGHT

After Moses' death, God gave the command of Israel to Joshua. These were the words God spoke to Joshua at the beginning of his leadership:

---

[95] Deuteronomy 6:1-12

> Be strong and of good courage, for to this people you shall divide as an inheritance the land which I swore to their fathers to give them. Only be strong and very courageous, that you may ***observe*** to do according to all the law which Moses My servant commanded you; do not turn from it to the right hand or to the left, that you may prosper wherever you go. This Book of the Law shall not depart from your mouth, but you shall ***meditate*** in it day and night, that you may observe to do according to all that is written in it. For then you will make your way prosperous, and then you will have good success.[96]

The theme of prosperity, success, and God's presence is again brought up as it was with Moses, and as it will be with David. This is not prosperity so God's people can simply enjoy riches. There is nothing wrong with having money, but the biblical meaning of prosperity does not have to do with excess of riches rather it is the prosperity and success of going deeper into God's presence and entering in to all the things God has designed for our lives. It is the prosperity and success of advancing His Kingdom and accomplishing His purposes for our lives as Moses and Joshua did. Yet

---

[96] Joshua 1:6-8

this success depends upon meditating and stewarding God's Word in our lives.

STEWARDING THE LIGHT

God told Joshua to "observe" all that is written in the Law. The Hebrew word for observe is "shamar." Joshua was to *shamar* the Law of God in his own life and it would then reflect in his governance over Israel and in the ultimate outcomes of his leadership.

As surely as God has filled us with the light of His Word we are to steward it. When God placed Adam in the Garden of Eden with rulership over all of it for the purpose of "tending" (or working; serving) and "keeping" it. The Hebrew word for "tending" is "abad," which carries in it priestly overtones of worship, just as the priests were to "abad" the Tabernacle of God.[97] Adam's life in the Garden, the discovery of God's good creation and his care for it were his worship. Adam was to do to the Garden as God Himself would have done.

Adam was to also "keep" the Garden, which in the Hebrew the word is "shamar." Shamar is used throughout the Old Testament as preserve; heed; protect; watch; save—but it is primarily used to

---

[97] For example, in Numbers 8:11 the Levites were to "perform (abad) the work of the Lord" in all their priestly and levitical functions.

keep or guard someone or something. The meaning of the word is to cause a condition to remain. Though the Bible never specifically uses the term "stewardship," the essence of "shamar" is that Adam was a steward of God's creation, the Garden, and the Word God had given to him. Adam was to worship the Lord by serving His creation and tending to its needs and causing it to grow into its full beauty—indeed, he was to care for the creation as God Himself cares for each of us.

Each of us has been placed in our own Garden with the same instructions from the Lord: to serve Him and others, and to steward all He has given to us so every part of our lives may flourish to its fullest potential. This has immense meaning for us all. God has given us a garden replete with beauty, gifts, and life. We have our own bodies, minds, and opportunities to steward. We have relationships with family, friends, and co-workers that need our stewarding. We have money and physical things that need stewarding as well. We are to do to everything in our garden what God Himself would do to make it beautiful and prosperous. When we do not take care of our homes, finances, things, or loved ones, we are not tending and stewarding what God gave us in our gardens.

The stewardship of "shamar" goes beyond our garden. 364 times in the Bible shamar is translated "keep, observe, heed" and most of the time it is used in the context of God's Word and Commandments to His people. Not only are we to listen to God's Word, we are to steward it in our lives. How is this done? It is simply obeying what we learn from it. When we hear, heed, and implement the Light of God's Word in our lives, we will live out the full beauty and richness His Word provides. But this does not happen on accident. This happens from careful and intentional stewardship if His Word.

As God said to Joshua, as He did with Moses and David, prosperity, fruitfulness, growth, understanding, wisdom, life, and God's close presence is based first and foremost on how we observe, meditate on, feed on, and steward God's Word in our own lives. As we spoke about earlier in the book, if the seed of God's Word is allowed to take root, it will reproduce itself into your Garden and your stewarding of God's Word will cause you to look more and more like Him.

DAVID: MEDITATE THE LIGHT

Though considerable arguments could be made for other individuals, David is possibly the man in the Bible who had the most intimate relationship with God. When we look closely at his Psalms, we see an unrivaled passion and intimacy with God. This same David wrote Psalm 1. In the composition and compiling of the book of Psalms, this first Psalm was not put here by accident, by chance, or by mistake. Everything God does, He does with great purpose and intentionality. The Holy Spirit is a master strategist. Though we looked at portions of this Psalm in depth earlier, I would like us to take one more look at it in the context of meditation. The opening words of the book of the Bible that most teaches us intimacy with God are these:

> Blessed *is* the man
> Who walks not in the counsel of the ungodly, nor stands in the path of sinners, nor sits in the seat of the scornful;
> But his delight *is* in the law of the LORD,
> And in His law he ***meditates*** day and night.
> He shall be like a tree planted by the rivers of water, that brings forth its fruit in its season, whose leaf also shall not wither;
> and whatever he does shall prosper.[98]

In short, David says if we will keep ourselves from sin and meditate on God's Word, then we will be spiritually vibrant, growing, and successful. This is reminiscent of Jesus' words, "…I chose you and appointed you that you should go and bear fruit and that your fruit should remain."[99] The key to a

---

[98] Psalm 1:1-3
[99] John 15:16

fruitful life is total dedication to the Lord and total adherence to His Word. If you desire a deeper relationship with God, you would do well to simply to these two things.

DEFINE MEDITATION

David speaks of meditating on God's Word. The general concept of meditation that most people have is that of a priest or monk of some eastern religion sitting is a cross-legged position chanting some mantras or trying to clear their mind to find inner peace and become one with the universe. This is not what we are talking about. That is another subject entirely. Suffice it to say that if you quiet your mind and focus on Jesus (see Colossians 3:2 and Galatians 5:16), you can connect with Him. But if you are not connected to Jesus in the spirit, you are opening yourself up to spiritual forces of darkness that will only deceive you.

The type of meditation David talks about is more clearly defined by the Hebrew term *hagah*, which is used in a variety of different ways: meditate, mourn, speak, utter, imagine, study, mutter, talk, roar, groan, or muse.

Meditation on God's Word is like a cow chewing its cud over and over again. The cow swallows, regurgitates and continues to chew until it has extracted every bit of nutrients out of the food.

Meditation on God's Word is the intentional and disciplined practice of thinking about, ruminating on, mulling over, and asking questions of what we read in the Bible. It includes talking about it, conversing with others on it, praying over it, studying it, and committing it to memory. It is going over it again and again, as Moses said, "when you sit in your house, when you walk by the way, when you lie down, and when you rise up." When you are driving in the car, it is remembering something intriguing you read in the Bible and turning it over in your mind.

In fact, the book of Proverbs tells us the same. At the very beginning of the book, Solomon gives the reason for his writing these sayings, proverbs, parables, and riddles:

> A wise man will hear and increase learning, and a man of understanding will attain wise counsel, to understand a proverb and an enigma, the words of the wise and their riddles.[100]

In other words, Solomon is saying if you will do more than simply read these proverbs and parables, if you will treat each saying as a riddle, learn to listen, think, and decipher it, it will act as a key to

---

[100] Proverbs 1:5-6

unlock a room of treasures. Each proverb is a different key. Use them and they will make you wise. This is meditating on God's Word.

The Hebrew word also speaks of muttering. You may not like to admit it, but you most likely talk to yourself out loud when you are alone. I confess there are moments when I am alone when I will work out a passage of Scripture out loud. Here is an actual conversation that I had "muttering" to myself one day:

"In John 3, Jesus said that what is born of the Spirit is spirit and what is born of flesh is flesh. Now I know Jesus was talking to Nicodemus about the need to be 'born again' by God's Spirit. But it seems to me that this is a spiritual principle that goes beyond our salvation alone. I remember that Jesus told the woman at the well in John 4 that those who worship God will worship Him in <u>spirit</u> and in truth. I also recognize that Galatians 5:16 says that if we walk in the spirit, we will not do the things the sinful flesh wants to do. Therefore, if I walk according to God's Spirit and in the spirit God has put in me, then I will get the things that the Spirit of God gives, but if I walk in my own flesh, then I will get the things that come from my flesh and that are born of my own sinfulness and weakness—that can't be good! Lord, teach me more to walk from my spirit being connected to Your

Spirit! Help me to have self-control to control my body and my mind (flesh) to be subjected to my spirit as I am lead by Your Holy Spirit like the Bible says in Philippians 4:8-9! Show me the things of the Spirit!"

ESTABLISHED THOUGHTS

Those are some good thoughts, and the deeper you go, the more you begin to uncover. Meditating on God's Word is not a cursory or quick reading to fulfill the obligation of a daily devotion. Meditating on God's Word comes from a love for the light and a desire for it to fill you more completely. This is love, not obligation; relationship, not law; commitment, not contract; spiritual, not mental. As we continue to think on God's Word, we have another wonderful promise from Proverbs 16:3, "Commit your works to the Lord, and your thoughts will be established." When we commit ourselves to the Lord in the spirit, when we submit ourselves fully to Him, He will guide the things we think about and even see in our minds. As we ruminate on His Word, thoughts will pop into our heads and the direction and connection we make in the Scriptures will be guided by the Holy Spirit. Didn't Jesus say the Holy Spirit would teach us *all things*?[101]

If we will walk in the Light and Jesus is in the

---

[101] John 14:26

Light, then we "will be like a tree planted by streams of water," and our leaves will not wither nor will our fruit fail. This is an incredible promise. God guarantees that His Word, like fertilizer, sunlight, and water, will give us everything we need to flourish at every time, season, place, and situation of life in which we find ourselves.

DAVID: MEDITATING THE MIRACULOUS

David continues to develop our understanding of meditating on God's Word and what it produces in our lives:

> I will *meditate* on the glorious splendor of Your majesty, and on Your wondrous works.[102]

David gives us a different spin on meditating God's Word—he says to meditate on God's amazing works. What amazing works are these, and where do we find them? We find them in many places. First of all, in God's Word. God is the God of miracles. We are directed to specifically think about the God of miracles, His amazing power, and the supernatural power He has worked. But the God of miracles of yesterday is the same God of miracles today.[103]

---

[102] Psalm 145:5
[103] Hebrews 13:8

We also hear of God's wondrous works in people's testimonies: when God provides supernaturally, when someone is spared from death, when someone is healed from disease, when God provides a way out of a difficult or impossible situation…the testimonies are endless. There is a reason why we are told to meditate on these things, and the key is found in the Hebrew.

The Hebrew word in this verse is rendered "meditate" in English, but in the Hebrew it is different. It is the word "siyach." The usage of this word is typically translated as "meditate, talk, pray, or declare." However, the root of this word is "to germinate; to sprout buds and shoots."

Testimonies are powerful. They connect our faith to God's ability to work miracles. We have already discussed at length how God's Word is seed and how we are to receive the "implanted Word" and how the seed of God's Word reproduces according to its own kind. God's work and God's Word are not separate from each other. Faith comes by hearing God's Word—or, to say it another way, the hearing of God's Word and works induces faith.[104]

There is a reason why Jesus did not simply walk around healing people. He preached the Kingdom.

---

[104] Romans 10:17

He preached the power and possibilities of the Father. He taught people who God is—and *then* He demonstrated it in power. Why? Because the hearing of the Word produces faith. Maybe you are making the observation that there were many times Jesus healed and did not preach. True. But how many people *heard* and *saw* and *experienced* His teaching and miracles and then went and *told* their testimonies? Didn't all the surrounding areas hear of Jesus before He even got there? The power of testimonies. The people had heard and their faith was already soaring into the heavens which is why when people knew Jesus was in the area they brought to Him all their sick and demon possessed.

There needs to be revelation before fulfillment. Meditating on God's Word and His wondrous deeds builds an atmosphere of faith where God can begin to work the impossible. Many times things of this nature will come to our minds, or we will suddenly hear a testimony, or read a Scripture—we begin to meditate on things we believe to be happenstance are actually orchestrated by the Holy Spirit who establishes our thoughts. He does this because it is the very thing He is getting ready to do ***now***, and He is preparing our faith as the atmosphere where He can display His miracles in our lives. In order for there to be fruit, there must be first a germinating seed, and that comes by hearing God's Word. Walking in the Light of God's Word, Spirit, and works will shine into us and through our lives in many spectacular ways—we will be walking in the miraculous and experience these amazing graces of God!

MEDITATE AGAIN AND AGAIN

I find that come Christmas and Easter, as a pastor, it is somewhat difficult to preach. Every year it is the same story on Easter Sunday, and every Christmas it is the same story for an entire month! I have heard, studied, preached, read, seen movies, and listened to just about every variation of these stories, yet we pastors have to try and find some different adaptation and perspective of the story to keep it fresh.

Yet the greatest miracle ever done is God becoming flesh; the Creator becoming His creation; and what is more, that the Holy One would become sin for us.[105] We know the story, but it is unfathomable for us to grasp exactly what this looked like for God and what all the beings of Heaven witnessed, seeing the Creator put on human flesh, die, and take our sins upon His holy, unsullied self. Psalm 111:2-4 gives insight into God's great works and our meditation of His Word:

---

[105] 2 Corinthians 5:21

The works of the LORD are great,
***studied** [sought for]* by all who have pleasure
in them. His work is honorable and glorious,
and His righteousness endures forever. He has
made His wonderful works to be **remembered**;
The LORD is gracious and full of compassion.

The word *studied* in the Hebrew is *darash*.
This word means to frequent a place; to seek out
and inquire; to trample with the feet so many times
that it makes a rut. This word is found several times
in the Psalms in conjunction with seeking God's
presence.

God's presence is to be frequently sought and
entered into. In the concept presented here in Psalm
111:2, we are to frequently replay in our minds all
the good things God has done; to walk down these
paths of reading, hearing, thinking about, and
studying until they are a rut in our hearts; they
become something that is deeply engrained in us.
His miracles are to be visited over and over again
until they are engraved into our lives marking them
in such a way they become part of us. Like a
blacksmith forming metal, the wondrous works of
God are hammered into our being and stamped into
our soul strengthening our faith. These works of
God are to be studied, searched out, revisited,
meditated and it forms our lives into the image of
Jesus Christ.

When I first discovered this truth of meditating on God's wondrous works, I thought, "that's what we do at Christmas and Easter!" It is not that the stories are tired and "played," but there must be a constant reminder of who God is and what He does, and the two times per year we replay God's greatest miracles which most rightly display His character—the humility of coming as a baby, His sacrifice in dying on the Cross, and His power in the resurrection—is Christmas and Easter.

REMEMBER
In Psalm 111:4, there is a second concept the author uses along with the engraving of God's works in our hearts is that of remembrance. The Hebrew word employed here is *zeker*, which literally means to make a memorial to commemorate something. When an Olympian wins the gold medal; a team wins the state championship trophy; a soldier receives the Medal of Honor, or there is some other award of honor or achievement, these things are memorials. They are the remembrance of a great work done or a astounding victory.

When I was ten years old I was diagnosed with bone marrow cancer in my right leg. As a fifth-grader, I went through a barrage of tests, which are difficult for anyone, but it wrenches the heart to see any child go through such long and painful testing.

The doctors knew it was cancer. Unknown to me at the time, they were considering the possibility of amputating my leg. Then the God of wonders showed up in my life. My church prayed for me and God touched me—my leg was healed! I still went through a biopsy procedure, but the doctors were completely astounded that no cancer was found.

After the several months-long ordeal which was very painful and emotional, my parents presented me with a little trophy. On the plaque at the foot of the trophy is inscribed, "Overcoming adversity." Every time I see it, I remember. I remember that I still have my leg. I remember what I went through. I remember God's faithfulness and healing power. It is a memorial to God's great works.

After Joshua took command of Israel, the first thing that happened was a great miracle. The Jordan River stood between the Israelites and the Promised Land, just as with Moses, the Red Sea stood between the Israelites and their freedom. God split the sea for Moses, and then split the river for Joshua. Upon reaching the other side, God told Joshua to take twelve stones from the middle of the river and set them up as a memorial to God's power and faithfulness, so that when future generations looked at it, they would hear the story—they would remember.[106]

This is why we have Christmas trees! They are memorials. The tree is an Evergreen—representing leaves that do not wither and there is always life. We decorate them with lights, reminding us that Jesus is the Light of the world. There is usually a star or an angel on top of the tree because both those things show up in the Christmas story, and both direct people toward Jesus. There are gifts under the tree which should remind us of God's greatest gift of salvation to us.

Every Christmas and Easter we revisit, study, and remember these stories again and again because the God of yesterday is the God of today. The God of miracles is the God of today. The God of life is the God of today. He makes us remember His wonders because everything He says and does are intentional and purpose-filled. His works are not for a show but to release life and make an impact on our lives that lasts far beyond the initial event. His miracles are like a pebble in a pond—an initial event widening into greater and great influence. Such are the incarnation and the resurrection: initial events that have rippled out to change everything in our world. But all of God's miracles do that. They certainly help people, but they are signs that point to Jesus which ripple out to change *your world* and the

---

[106] Joshua 4:1-7

people in it.

As we remember His wonders, we remember His power, goodness, and love for us—we remember that the God of wonders continues His wonders today. Revisiting and remember gives us "faith for today and bright hope for tomorrow."

11
THE LIGHT AND OUR WORSHIP

When the Israelites were in the desert after their liberation from slavery in Egypt, God gave them the most precious gift of His Word. He entrusted it to them with the end result in mind of them living out that Word in their hearts and daily lives; *they were to become God's Word itself—the Light of the world.* God's Word and Light were to define them. God's Word and light were to transform them. God's Word and light were to lead them. God's Word and light were to sustain them. God's Word and light were to be lived through their lives so all the nations around them would see God's glory. They were to be the nation who incarnated God's Word.

As a sign and a test for them, God gave them bread from Heaven every morning called Manna. Manna was what sustained them in the desert. They were not to save any of the heavenly bread for the next day, except on one day of the week in preparation for the Sabbath. The reason was because they were to feed upon it daily as it was freshly provided from Heaven. Through the Manna, God was testing their obedience and teaching them the importance of depending on Him for everything they needed. Moses also instructed the people regarding Manna saying the Lord gave it to them so they would learn that "man does not live by bread alone but by every Word that comes from the mouth of God."[107]

God's Word was physically represented by bread. As bread feeds and sustains the body, God's Word feeds and sustains our souls and spirits. As God gave the bread, so His instructions for life are given in His Word. As God gave the bread on a daily basis, we are to feed upon His Word on a daily basis. As the nutrients of bread cause the body to grow, God's Word causes our spiritual lives to grow.

GOD'S SPEAKING, CLEANSING WORD

Though God does place leaders in place to teach His Word,[108] nowhere does the Bible say that the people cannot search it for themselves—as a matter of fact, knowing God's Word and studying it is the key to righteous and effective living.[109] Also, the

---

[107] Deuteronomy 8:3
[108] See Psalm 119:130 and Leviticus 10:8-11
[109] See Psalm 1

Bereans in the book of Acts were commended for the way they searched the Scriptures for themselves in order to verify if what the preacher (the Apostle Paul) was saying was accurate.[110]

There is a maxim in rabbinical Judaism, which says, "When I pray, I talk to God. When I study the Scriptures, God talks to me." There is something supernatural that happens every time we come to God's Word. Through it, the Spirit speaks to us. Its power transforms us. Its pure truth cleanses us. Jesus "loved the church and gave Himself for her, that He might sanctify and cleanse her with the ***washing of water by the word.***"[111] Jesus also told His disciples that they were cleansed through the Word they had received from Him.[112] God is not interested in a Church that simply fills seats, He wants a Church that is functional, equipped, purified, and ready with His Word. How, then, is this possible if we do not know what His Word says about what He requires of us? Reading the Bible is essential to our growth as God's people.

SACRIFICE OF WORSHIP

Reading God's Word is the highest form of worship we can offer God. Some who might read these words may find them hard to digest but I would

---

[110] Acts 17:10-12
[111] Ephesians 5:25-26
[112] John 15:3

suggest to you that this comes from a faulty understanding of what worship truly is. Too many people perceive worship as the part of the church service where we either pray or sing to the Lord. I do not deny that such points of worship are honoring to the Lord, uplifting to our own spirits, help us to connect our spirits to God, and are very biblical in their expression. But worship, in its essence, is a sacrifice to the Lord.

Throughout the Old Testament, worship was offered to the Lord in the form of animal sacrifices. But the New Testament, having done away with animal sacrifices because of Jesus' better sacrifice on the cross, does not actually change in its understanding of worship. It is not as if sacrifices were "under the law" and now singing is "under grace." We are specifically instructed in the New Testament to give sacrifices. The Apostle Paul says, "I plead with you to *give your bodies* to God because of all he has done for you. Let them be *a living and holy sacrifice*—the kind he will find acceptable. This is truly the way to worship him.[113] Note that this is a <u>living</u> sacrifice, not a dead one!

If worship is a sacrifice, then what constitutes our worship? In short, *everything constitutes our worship*. Our singing to the Lord is a physical, emotional, mental, and spiritual sacrifice to the

---

[113] Romans 12:1 (New Living Translation)

Lord. We worship with our minds and our spirits as we sing. We offer our bodies to the Lord by simply *being* at church! Our bodies are also walking musical instruments that we offer to God. We have a wind instrument by our lungs. We have a stringed instrument by our vocal chords. We have percussion instruments as we clap our hands. Our worship includes coming to church and being with the Body of Christ.

Our worship is in giving with joyful hearts our tithes and offerings to the Lord. Giving in worship is not "tipping" God, nor giving as if it were some sort of tax imposed upon us by the Almighty. If your giving is done begrudgingly, then it is neither trust in God's faithfulness, nor an act of worship. Worship is taking care of the people and things God has entrusted to us. Caring for our spouse and children as well as taking care of our houses and physical bodies are acts of worship. By using our things for honor and instructing people in the ways of the Lord, we are honoring God who gave them to us. Keeping ourselves pure from the impurities of this world and serving other people are also acts of worship to God.[114]

WORSHIP FORMS US

Our worship is also tied to the things to which we most serve. Our worship transforms us; we become

---

[114] James 1:27

precisely like the thing that we love and give ourselves to. Read carefully what the Psalm 115:3-8 says,

> But our God is in heaven; He does whatever He pleases. Their idols are silver and gold, the work of men's hands. They have mouths, but they do not speak; eyes they have, but they do not see; they have ears, but they do not hear; noses they have, but they do not smell; they have hands, but they do not handle; feet they have, but they do not walk; nor do they mutter through their throat. Those who make them are like them; so is everyone who trusts in them.

The Psalmist makes a hard distinction between the idols of the nations and our God. The idols of the nations have nothing of value to offer. They offer no relationship. They offer no practical help. They offer no spiritual insight. They have all the right things on the outside; they have the aspect of something good and helpful, but they, for all intents and purposes, are useless.

An idol is anything occupying the number one spot in our lives, and this can manifest through anything which we love the most in this world. Such love and devotion will inevitably transform us into the image of such objects of adoration—as the last line says,

"Those who make them are like them; so is everyone who trusts in them." If you love money more than anything else, you will become greedy and self-centered. You become like the thing you worship. Jesus instructs us saying that our heart will be wherever our treasure is.[115] It is easy to figure out what a person's treasure is: it is where they spend the most time, the most money, and the most love. It is strange how busy people are, yet they seem to have time for their job, and everything else that is perceived to be fun, exciting, and stimulating, but when it comes to Sunday morning, all of a sudden "I'm too tired." The simple fact is your physical body, with all its affections, will be where your actual treasure lies. When Israel was finally punished by God and sent into exile in Babylon, the Bible says their judgment came about because, "They worshiped worthless idols, so they became worthless themselves."[116] Because of misplaced worship, which is idolatry, we become useless to the Kingdom of God.

There is real danger in what we choose to set before us. However innocently we perceive our internet, Facebook, Instagram, or Twitter usage, or the programs we choose to binge watch, or the music we pump into our souls 24/7, all those things begin

---

[115] Matthew 6:21
[116] 2 Kings 17:15

to transform us into its own image. We get addicted to it because we are worshipping at its altar.

Have you ever been to a concert? Don't tell me that's not worship! Everyone excited to be there, paying a high price with both money and time just to be there. Everyone is jumping, screaming, hands waving, and singing along with all the songs. Yet in church, before the King of the Universe, those same people seem to have a hard time keeping their eyes open offering nothing of themselves to God—if ever they decide to even show up to church. *This is not because church is boring—it is because God's presence is not their treasure, therefore their heart is not there.* God does not desire lip service worship. He desires worship from the heart. Jesus said of His own generation that they honor God with their lips, but their heart is far from Him.[117]

There was a time in my life when I was really in to a specific TV show that had lots of cursing in it. I would faithfully watch it, and anticipate the next episode. The curses were always *beeped* out, but who are they fooling? We all know exactly what they are saying. After a time, I noticed a change in me. Though I did not use curse words, one would slip out every now and again. But what was more frightening to me was that every time I was irritated or angry, a fountain of cursing would run through

---

[117] Matthew 15:8

my mind even if the words did not make it out of my lips. The thing I was spending so much time with was slowly transforming me. I ended up cutting off that show, and others like it, from my TV habits, and I needed prayer to break the power of cursing over my life.

The devil works overtime to distort our worship through distractions and stealing our affections. Put in front of yourself the kinds of things that you want to become. Many people do not desire to become cheaters and liars, but they don't seem to have a problem watching them on TV. It is as if a person who knows these things are wrong and doesn't want to displease God by living this way, lives vicariously through the character portrayed, because secretly, there is still some adventurous desire for these things. We know it is not okay to live these things in our lives, but it is ok to let them live in the mind; in our secret life? Be careful. And just because a particular sin doesn't *manifest* itself physically in your life doesn't mean it is not *present*. Perhaps we have not murdered anyone physically, but Jesus said anger toward someone in your secret life is the sin of murder. When we stand before the Lord, He will not only judge our actions, but our secret lives, too.[118]

If we want to become more like God, then we need

---

[118] Romans 2:16

to put His Word in front of us. Worship Him. Not only will you become like the things you worship, but you will also develop a taste for them. It is sweeter than honey[119] and the wisdom of God found in it is worth more than costly jewels.[120] Yet it is this treasure that, when implemented, will change everything about us, our families, our jobs, our mentalities into the image of God—and our lives will be lived in the way God intended them to be lived, and we will experience His full goodness, health, and blessings. Yet how can we live in His full blessings when we don't know His Word? How can we play a sport if we have no knowledge of the rules? How can we know what sin is unless the transforming Word of God teaches us?

When we fill ourselves up with the knowledge of the Lord, all other desires will pale in comparison to His goodness, purity, truth, and life. God's Word is the greatest treasure. In the words of the old song, "Turn your eyes upon Jesus. Look full in His wonderful face, and the things of earth will grow strangely dim in the light of His glory and grace."

WORSHIP AND THE WORD

My wife and I have four children. We are doing our best to raise them in the ways of the Lord, to teach them to honor and respect both God and us, and to

---

[119] Psalm 119:103
[120] Psalm 19:10; Proverbs 8:11

trust us when we speak. The Bible says that we are to honor our parents,[121] and the best way my children can honor my wife and me is through their listening and obedience to us. For instance, it is honoring when I tell them to clean their room, and they do it with a happy attitude. Then there are other times when I will say to them, "Everyone, put your shoes on!" And the immediate question is, "Why?" Admittedly, that is not a horrible thing to ask, and they don't do it disrespectfully, but in the moment, the "why" is not the issue. It is the fact that dad has spoken, and dad knows what is going on, and dad needs the kids to trust him and obey—everything else will be explained in due time.

Though we do permit and encourage healthy dialogue when situations or questions arise, my wife and I do not allow for dismissive attitudes, belligerent arguing, disrespectful tantrums, or cool passivity. There is a way to ask questions and open dialogues yet honor those in authority, and on the other hand there is the rebellious, selfish spirit that honors one's self and dishonors those whom God has placed in authority over us.

The best way to respect our parents is by obeying them, not speaking badly of them, helping them, etc. Yet we have more than earthly parents, we also have a heavenly Father. I suspect that the

---

[121] Exodus 20:12

Commandment to "honor our father and our mother" has implications for our relationship to God, as well. Listen to what Jesus said regarding listening and obeying:

> Therefore whoever hears these sayings of Mine, and does them, I will liken him to a wise man who built his house on the rock: and the rain descended, the floods came, and the winds blew and beat on that house; and it did not fall, for it was founded on the rock. "But everyone who hears these sayings of Mine, and does not do them, will be like a foolish man who built his house on the sand: and the rain descended, the floods came, and the winds blew and beat on that house; and it fell. And great was its fall."[122]

Both people in this parable <u>heard</u> the same word. The difference between the two is not who heard or did not hear, or to put it in another context, the difference is not those who read their Bibles and those who did not; those who went to church and those who did not; those who heard the preacher and those who did not—this is not the difference. The parable is clear: both heard the Word. The difference is the one who put the Word into practice and the one who did not.

Just because we go to church does not guarantee our

---

[122] Matthew 7:24-27

lives are not going to fall. Just because we read the Bible does not mean that our lives are not going to be ruined.

I have known people who have served the Lord for years, gone to great churches for decades, yet they wandered away from the faith and somehow or another, their lives fell apart. How is this possible? It is not good enough to say they never truly believed. The fact is, they *did* believe. One needs not only hear, but have the spiritual discernment, diligence, and dependence upon the Lord to begin to apply the principles of the Word of God to everyday living. Every person has to approach the Word of God expecting to be changed, asking God to transform them, and then living out the changes outside the church services.

Too many people—many of them well intentioned who have genuine love for God—come to the Bible with their own convenient bias saying, "I like this verse, but I do not like that one…this part makes me feel good, but that part challenges me in ways I don't like." They distort God's Word and twist it fit into their own favorite ways of living while fooling themselves into thinking that they are living for God and obeying His Word. The best way we can worship and honor God is by hearing His Word, letting it straighten us out and change us into His image and then live it out back to Him. What better way to honor and worship God by taking time with His Word and then loving Him by living it?

WORSHIP AND OBEDIENCE

The Lord sent the prophet Samuel to Saul, the first king of Israel. God, through Samuel, had instructed Saul to fight against a certain city, and all the animals along with the city were to be destroyed. After Saul's glorious victory, Samuel came to greet him. Though I am taking a bit of imaginative freedom with the biblical text, I'll bet their conversation went something like this:[123]

"Samuel! So great to see you! I am glad you're here. I have done everything God asked of me."

"Are you sure?" asked Samuel.

"Sure am."

"Then why do I hear cattle and sheep when you were asked by God to destroy them?"

"Well, get this, Samuel…you're gonna love it. I did *mostly* what God asked of me. I figured it would be a waste to kill all the animals. So I decided…I know this sounds a little funny…but I had a great idea that I think even God would be proud of. Come to think of it, I wonder why God didn't think of this first…but here it is: I saved some animals to give to

---

[123] See 1 Samuel 15:12-15

God in sacrifice! God's likes sacrifices, right? I know He does. So it doesn't matter that I made a few amendments to His Word—because I am going to honor Him with sacrifices."

Samuel replied, *"Has the Lord as great delight in burnt offerings and sacrifices, as in obeying the voice of the Lord? Behold, to obey is better than sacrifice, and to heed than the fat of rams."*[124]

Everyone of us has lived this same situation before the Lord. It is like sending a child to clean his room. How does he clean it? By shoving everything under the bed and into the closet. When mom or dad goes to check the room, at first glance in looks great! Upon further inspection, the closet door gets opened and the parent is inundated with the mess. The mess just moved from an open place to a hidden place. The child insists they did a good job. But the task was to *clean* the room, not move the mess from one place to another. The child then maintains that he at least made the place look good, but we know it doesn't work that way. This was the kind of worship Saul offered to the Lord. It was worship on his terms and at his convenience. As a matter of fact, later on in the story, we learn that one of the reasons for Saul's disobedience was he "feared the voice of the people and obeyed their voice."[125]

---

[124] 1 Samuel 15:22
[125] 1 Samule 15:24

The sacrifice of worship is never on our own terms, it is based on what God requires of us. Samuel was basically saying to Saul that God doesn't care about his "sacrifices." Did you hear that? God is uninterested in what we have to offer if it is not what He requires of us. If God wanted certain "sacrifices" of religiosity from us, He would ask. Jesus said to the Pharisees of His day, "What sorrow awaits you teachers of religious law and you Pharisees. Hypocrites! For you are careful to tithe even the tiniest income from your herb gardens, but you ignore the more important aspects of the law—justice, mercy, and faith. You should tithe, yes, but do not neglect the more important things."[126]

What are the sacrifices that most please the Lord? What can we give to Him that He did not first give to us? The sacrifice He loves is an issue of the heart, an issue ridding ourselves of self-will and rebellion, and an issue of humility and obedience. In the offering of proper worship sacrifices to the Lord, the Psalm says,

> Will I eat the flesh of bulls, Or drink the blood of goats? Offer to God **thanksgiving**, and **pay your vows** to the Most High. **Call upon Me** in the day of trouble; I will deliver you, and you shall glorify Me…Whoever offers praise

---

[126] Matthew 23:23 (New Living Translation)

glorifies Me; and to him who orders his conduct aright I will show the salvation of God."[127]

What we can give God in our sacrifices of worship is:

1) Gratitude. Our gratitude is best expressed in living righteously according to His Word.

2) Faithfulness. The Psalm says to "pay your vows." In other words, do what you said you were going to do for the Lord. We can offer a sacrifice of faithfulness to Him.

3) Trust. We can honor God with the sacrifice of trust by calling on Him in the hour of our need instead of depending upon our own strength. God is not interested in our things, our sacrifices, our displays of religiosity—He wants faithfulness, love, respect, obedience, trust, and thankfulness. All of these things can be lived out because of understanding of God's Word. Reading, studying, and living out God's Word is the way in which we can ultimately best worship God. Read carefully one more time Psalm 119:1-7:

> Joyful are people of integrity,
> who follow the instructions of the Lord.
> Joyful are those who obey his laws

---

[127] Psalm 50:13-15; 23

and search for him with all their hearts.
They do not compromise with evil,
and they walk only in his paths.
You have charged us
to keep your commandments carefully.
***Oh, that my actions would consistently
reflect your decrees!
Then I will not be ashamed
when I compare my life with your commands.***
As I learn your righteous regulations,
I will thank you by living as I should![128]

---

[128] Psalm 119:1-7 (New Living Translation)

ABOUT THE AUTHOR

Kyle W. Bauer has a rich ministry history spanning nearly two decades. Throughout his career, he's served as a children's pastor, a church planter, a missionary in Mexico, and a professor of ministry and history at the King's University and at La Facultad de Teología. His current ministry assignment is serving as the senior pastor at Pathway, in Northridge, CA. Kyle holds a Bachelor's Degree in Theological Studies and a Master's Degree in Divinity, both from The King's University. He and his wife, Teresa, were married in 2003 and have four children—three boys, and one girl.

For more information or to contact Kyle, you can visit his site www.kwbauer.com

His books are available in English and Spanish at www.amazon.com

www.ingramcontent.com/pod-product-compliance
Lightning Source LLC
Chambersburg PA
CBHW031445040426
42444CB00007B/978